JUMBLE®

Theater

These Puzzles Deserve a Curtain Call!

T0096051

Henri Arnold,
Bob Lee,
Mike Argirion,
Jeff Knurek, &
David L. Hoyt

TRIUMPH
BOOKS

This book is available in quantity at special discounts
for your group or organization.

For further information, contact:

Triumph Books LLC
814 North Franklin Street
Chicago, Illinois 60610
Phone: (312) 337-0747
www.triumphbooks.com

Printed in U.S.A.

ISBN: 978-1-62937-484-0

Design by Sue Knopf

Contents

JUMBLE®

Theater

*Classic
Puzzles*

Unscramble these four Jumbles, one letter
to each square, to form four ordinary words.

RUYRH

GUHRS

NERTEL

NADRIC

Mario's

Wow!
Look at
her.

You
haven't
stopped.

THE CYCLOPS COULDN'T
HELP BUT NOTICE THE
NEW ARRIVAL AFTER
SHE ----

Now arrange the circled letters to form
the surprise answer, as suggested by the
above cartoon.

*Print
answer
here*

JUMBLE®

Unscramble these four Jumbles, one letter
to each square, to form four ordinary words.

KAKIH

CANTE

EENAVU

XPULED

Go! Don't let him catch up!

IF ICHABOD CRANE WAS
GOING TO OUTRUN SLEEPY
HOLLOW'S HORSEMAN, HE'D
NEED TO ---

Now arrange the circled letters to form
the surprise answer, as suggested by the
above cartoon.

Print answer here

JUMBLE®

Unscramble these four Jumbles, one letter to each square, to form four ordinary words.

VEAWE

TINNH

FLUCPU

TOYNTK

How about, He wanted to..."SEIZE-HER" SALAD?

We did that last year. What if we ask our Facebook fans?

f JUMBLE

WE COULDN'T COME UP WITH A NEW SALAD PUN ... IF YOU HAVE A GOOD ONE —––

Now arrange the circled letters to form the surprise answer, as suggested by the above cartoon.

Print answer here " ⬡⬡⬡⬡⬡⬡⬡ " ⬡⬡⬡⬡

JUMBLE®

Unscramble these four Jumbles, one letter
to each square, to form four ordinary words.

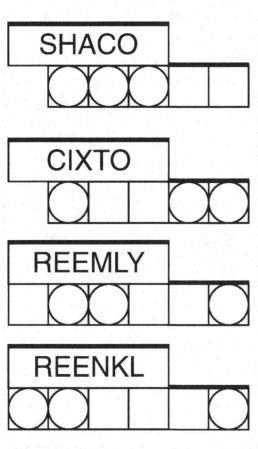

SHACO

CIXTO

REEMLY

REENKL

CHIPATI ...
WHOLE WHE
PIZZA ....

Why is this
so small?

That's life, kid.
It's called
taxes.

PIZZA
BOB'S

IT WAS FINALLY PAYDAY
AND THE NEW EMPLOYEE
GOT A --

Now arrange the circled letters to form
the surprise answer, as suggested by the
above cartoon.

*Print
answer
here*

JUMBLE®

Unscramble these four Jumbles, one letter
to each square, to form four ordinary words.

CROPH

RAVLA

DIRALA

WORDSY

So, why aren't we going with a four-way intersection?

My thesis showed that roundabouts are safer and more fuel efficient.

HE GRADUATED WITH A DEGREE IN STREET BUILDING WHICH MADE HIM A ----

Now arrange the circled letters to form
the surprise answer, as suggested by the
above cartoon.

Print answer here " ⬡⬡⬡⬡⬡ " ⬡⬡⬡⬡⬡⬡⬡⬡

JUMBLE®

Unscramble these four Jumbles, one letter
to each square, to form four ordinary words.

DABIE

TOLCH

ESUWIN

ROVYSA

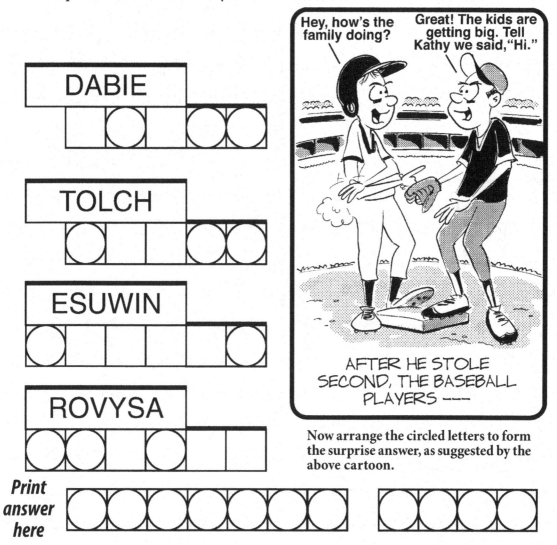

Hey, how's the
family doing?

Great! The kids are
getting big. Tell
Kathy we said, "Hi."

AFTER HE STOLE
SECOND, THE BASEBALL
PLAYERS ---

Now arrange the circled letters to form
the surprise answer, as suggested by the
above cartoon.

Print
answer
here

JUMBLE.

Unscramble these four Jumbles, one letter
to each square, to form four ordinary words.

CHONT

GNTIE

BIDSEE

TYRREA

Mornin' neighbors!

Where did all these people come from?

I wish we could live here longer than just the weekend.

THE CAMPGROUND'S POPULATION GOES UP WHEN PEOPLE BECOME ----

Now arrange the circled letters to form
the surprise answer, as suggested by the
above cartoon.

*Print
answer
here* " ⬡⬡⬡⬡⬡⬡⬡ - ⬡⬡⬡⬡⬡ "

JUMBLE®

Unscramble these four Jumbles, one letter
to each square, to form four ordinary words.

PDATA

ENDUC

MOLANS

LEYILK

Wow! I didn't think your allergies would be so bad here.

All these flowers are in bloom.

FIJI GARDEN

HER ALLERGIES WERE ACTING UP ON HER TROPICAL VACATION. SHE FELT LIKE SHE WAS IN ----

Now arrange the circled letters to form the surprise answer, as suggested by the above cartoon.

Print answer here " ◯◯◯◯◯◯ - ◯◯◯◯ "

JUMBLE®

Unscramble these four Jumbles, one letter to each square, to form four ordinary words.

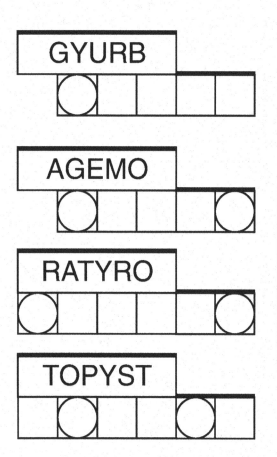

GYURB

AGEMO

RATYRO

TOPYST

Take thy beak from out my heart, and take thy form from off my door!

Nevermore.

WHEN THE MACAWS PUT ON A PLAY, IT WAS A —

Now arrange the circled letters to form the surprise answer, as suggested by the above cartoon.

Print answer here "◯◯◯◯◯◯◯"

JUMBLE®

Unscramble these four Jumbles, one letter to each square, to form four ordinary words.

PODTA

PITNE

SNELOS

DAILNN

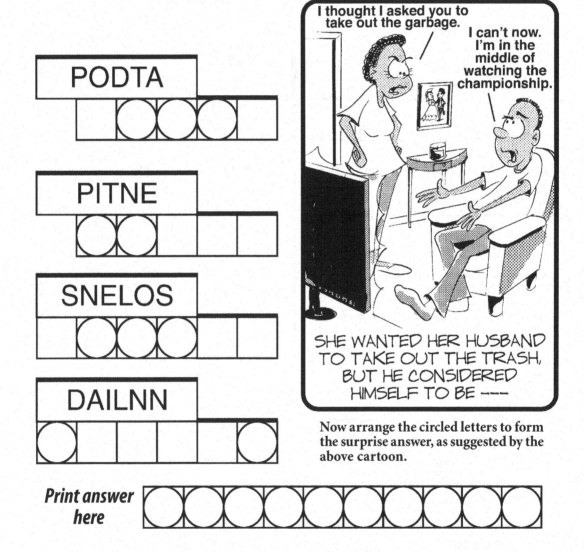

I thought I asked you to take out the garbage.

I can't now. I'm in the middle of watching the championship.

SHE WANTED HER HUSBAND TO TAKE OUT THE TRASH, BUT HE CONSIDERED HIMSELF TO BE ----

Now arrange the circled letters to form the surprise answer, as suggested by the above cartoon.

Print answer here

JUMBLE®

Unscramble these four Jumbles, one letter
to each square, to form four ordinary words.

LYCCE

LYOHL

CRADEA

NATBOY

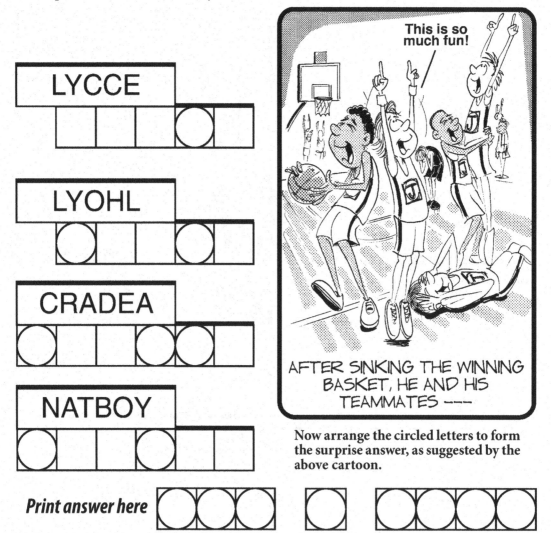

This is so
much fun!

AFTER SINKING THE WINNING
BASKET, HE AND HIS
TEAMMATES ———

Now arrange the circled letters to form
the surprise answer, as suggested by the
above cartoon.

Print answer here

JUMBLE®

Unscramble these four Jumbles, one letter
to each square, to form four ordinary words.

TPEHD

GINAA

BLONOG

NAMEBO

Where are
your
gloves?

I'll have to
run home to
get them.

THE KIDS WANTED TO PLAY
BASEBALL, BUT THERE
WEREN'T ENOUGH
GLOVES ---

Now arrange the circled letters to form
the surprise answer, as suggested by the
above cartoon.

Print answer here

13

JUMBLE®

Unscramble these four Jumbles, one letter
to each square, to form four ordinary words.

PEOMT

RADYT

MOSYRT

VLARGE

The butcher gives out scraps.
The baker gives away muffins.
The steakhouse will give us bones.

Gee, Spike.
You know
everything!

THE DOG KNEW WHICH
STORES TO GET SNACKS
AT BECAUSE HE WAS ----

Now arrange the circled letters to form
the surprise answer, as suggested by the
above cartoon.

*Print
answer
here* "⟨ ⟩⟨ ⟩⟨ ⟩⟨ ⟩⟨ ⟩" ⟨ ⟩⟨ ⟩⟨ ⟩⟨ ⟩⟨ ⟩

JUMBLE®

Unscramble these four Jumbles, one letter
to each square, to form four ordinary words.

EARAN

GEERV

TALUWO

SHIXNP

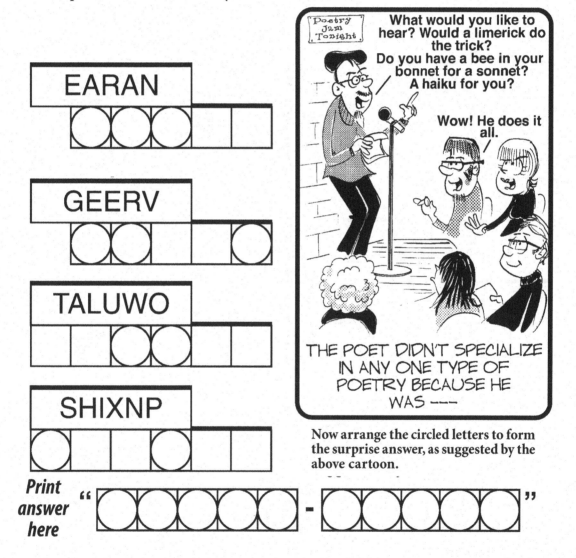

Poetry
Jam
Tonight

**What would you like to
hear? Would a limerick do
the trick?
Do you have a bee in your
bonnet for a sonnet?
A haiku for you?**

**Wow! He does it
all.**

THE POET DIDN'T SPECIALIZE
IN ANY ONE TYPE OF
POETRY BECAUSE HE
WAS ---

Now arrange the circled letters to form
the surprise answer, as suggested by the
above cartoon.

Print
answer
here

" ⬡⬡⬡⬡⬡ - ⬡⬡⬡⬡⬡ "

JUMBLE®

Unscramble these four Jumbles, one letter
to each square, to form four ordinary words.

GADEA

VEIRR

SEGNIN

VACIDE

THE GOLFERS LOVED THEIR
NEW ELECTRIC CAR,
ESPECIALLY ITS ----

Now arrange the circled letters to form
the surprise answer, as suggested by the
above cartoon.

*Print
answer
here*

JUMBLE®

Unscramble these four Jumbles, one letter to each square, to form four ordinary words.

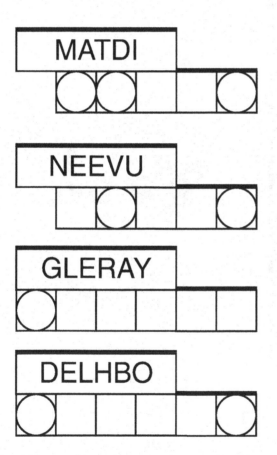

MATDI

NEEVU

GLERAY

DELHBO

Why aren't you out looking for brains?

I'm getting tired of you "living" off of us.

THE ZOMBIE COUPLE WORRIED THAT THEIR SON WAS BECOMING A ---

Now arrange the circled letters to form the surprise answer, as suggested by the above cartoon.

Print answer here

JUMBLE®

Unscramble these four Jumbles, one letter
to each square, to form four ordinary words.

DEBIA

PERIC

EVTLEV

YARRIT

Didn't they say, "No rain," this weekend?

They're never right.

THE WEATHER FORECAST
ENDED UP BEING INCORRECT,
WHICH WAS ----

Now arrange the circled letters to form
the surprise answer, as suggested by the
above cartoon.

Print answer here

JUMBLE®

Unscramble these four Jumbles, one letter
to each square, to form four ordinary words.

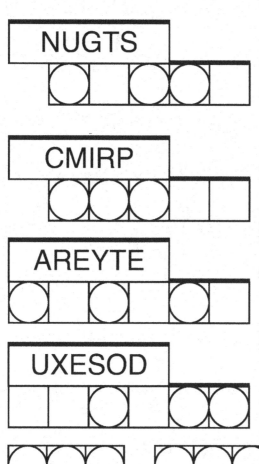

NUGTS

CMIRP

AREYTE

UXESOD

You still have
a fever! You
need to get
your rest.

Wait up. I'll get
my shoes on.

HE COULDN'T TRAIN FOR
THE MARATHON BECAUSE HIS
COLD HAD TO ----

Now arrange the circled letters to form
the surprise answer, as suggested by the
above cartoon.

*Print
answer
here*

JUMBLE®

Unscramble these four Jumbles, one letter to each square, to form four ordinary words.

HELIW

TAIRO

AAINUG

CICINO

Do you want another slice?

You need to fold it first.

For once, I'd like a full slice.

FOR THE FASHION MODEL, ALWAYS BEING ON A DIET AND COUNTING CALORIES WAS ---

Now arrange the circled letters to form the surprise answer, as suggested by the above cartoon.

Print answer here

JUMBLE®

Unscramble these four Jumbles, one letter to each square, to form four ordinary words.

SAYTE

KILYS

SIVTEN

LIPCEV

Take your time.

Do I get one?

I'm going to finish this right away.

SHE PLANNED ON FINISHING HER LOLLIPOP ---

Now arrange the circled letters to form the surprise answer, as suggested by the above cartoon.

Print answer here

21

JUMBLE®

Unscramble these four Jumbles, one letter
to each square, to form four ordinary words.

PRIEG

SSEEN

RURAPO

UDARSI

Wow! Things have changed.

Look at those modern buildings.

SINCE THEIR LAST TRIP TO THE CZECH REPUBLIC CAPITAL, THERE'D BEEN MUCH ----

Now arrange the circled letters to form
the surprise answer, as suggested by the
above cartoon.

Print answer here

" ◯◯◯◯◯◯ - ◯◯◯◯ "

JUMBLE®

Unscramble these four Jumbles, one letter
to each square, to form four ordinary words.

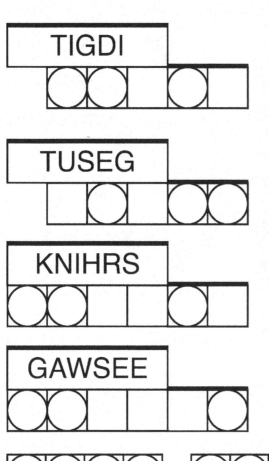

TIGDI

TUSEG

KNIHRS

GAWSEE

**Royal Flush Pays
$1 Million**

The next card is
the 10 of clubs.

That doesn't
work. I needed
the 10 of hearts!

HE WAS HOPING TO GET A
ROYAL FLUSH, BUT THE
CARDS DIDN'T QUITE ----

Now arrange the circled letters to form
the surprise answer, as suggested by the
above cartoon.

*Print
answer
here*

JUMBLE®

Unscramble these four Jumbles, one letter
to each square, to form four ordinary words.

GETAN

OYZDO

LEGFUN

HROTEB

I've got you, honey.
You need to relax.

There's nothing
to keep me from
going over. This
is so scary.

WHEN SHE REACHED THE
RIM OF THE GRAND CANYON,
SHE WAS ----

Now arrange the circled letters to form
the surprise answer, as suggested by the
above cartoon.

Print answer here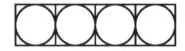

JUMBLE®

Unscramble these four Jumbles, one letter to each square, to form four ordinary words.

ROPEA

BNALD

RILGEL

RONCEE

I see you were second in your class in obedience school.

As you can see, I'm perfect for the job.

THE CANINE WANTED TO BE STATIONED BETWEEN CANADA AND THE U.S. BECAUSE HE WAS A ---

Now arrange the circled letters to form the surprise answer, as suggested by the above cartoon.

Print answer here

JUMBLE®

Unscramble these four Jumbles, one letter
to each square, to form four ordinary words.

VECOT

SEEEG

GLANTE

NUTICD

Behold! The Dandy Blade
3000. It has built-in Wi-Fi,
thermometer, thickness
gauge and more!

THE CHEF'S NEW
HIGH-TECH
KNIFE WAS ---

Now arrange the circled letters to form
the surprise answer, as suggested by the
above cartoon.

*Print
answer
here*

JUMBLE®

Theater

Daily
Puzzles

JUMBLE®

Unscramble these four Jumbles, one letter
to each square, to form four ordinary words.

COTHB

SIYRK

RIDCEN

GALEEL

What a neat day
this has been.

Great
waves.
Perfect
day.

THE SURFERS WERE HAVING
A WONDERFUL TIME.
EVERYTHING WAS ----

Now arrange the circled letters to form
the surprise answer, as suggested by the
above cartoon.

Print
answer
here

" ⬡⬡⬡⬡⬡⬡⬡ " - ⬡⬡⬡⬡

JUMBLE®

Unscramble these four Jumbles, one letter to each square, to form four ordinary words.

CREPH

ATAWI

DOSITU

TEYMSS

What do you ladies think?

The middle is so soft and chewy.

You aced these!

THE COOKIES SHAPED LIKE TENNIS RACKETS WERE A HIT. EVERYONE REALLY LIKED THEIR ---

Now arrange the circled letters to form the surprise answer, as suggested by the above cartoon.

Print answer here

29

JUMBLE®

Unscramble these four Jumbles, one letter
to each square, to form four ordinary words.

TEFON

SOKIK

NIUMEM

SICONU

Today's Guest JUMBLER is
LYNN JOHNSTON
creator of FOR BETTER OR FOR WORSE

FARLEY ROLLED ON THE
BARN FLOOR BECAUSE OF
HIS ----

Now arrange the circled letters to form
the surprise answer, as suggested by the
above cartoon.

Print answer
here " ☐☐ - ☐☐☐☐☐☐☐ "

JUMBLE®

Unscramble these four Jumbles, one letter to each square, to form four ordinary words.

ATULF

TINNH

GITHEW

MDAISY

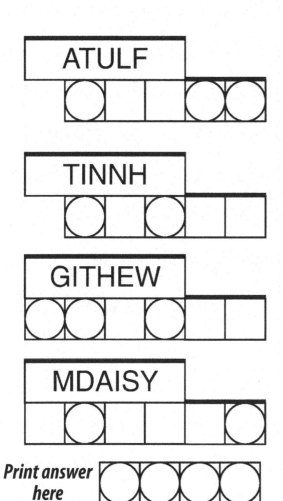

Hold on!

WHEN THE PLANE HIT TURBULENCE, EVERYTHING ---

Now arrange the circled letters to form the surprise answer, as suggested by the above cartoon.

Print answer here

JUMBLE®

Unscramble these four Jumbles, one letter to each square, to form four ordinary words.

NURKT

SERDS

KHANES

EEMCOB

TO PAINT THE SWIMMERS, THE ARTIST USED ---

Now arrange the circled letters to form the surprise answer, as suggested by the above cartoon.

Print answer here

JUMBLE®

Unscramble these four Jumbles, one letter
to each square, to form four ordinary words.

VURSI

VLATI

DEPRAA

NOPYLE

I hear that she eats kids.

I hear she turns them into mice.

"Sugar, spice and anything I can get. Eat these cookies and you will forget."

THERE WAS A RUMOR
GOING AROUND THAT SHE
WAS A WITCH...
SHE WANTED TO ---

Now arrange the circled letters to form
the surprise answer, as suggested by the
above cartoon.

Print answer "□◯◯◯◯◯◯◯" ◯◯
here

JUMBLE®

Unscramble these four Jumbles, one letter to each square, to form four ordinary words.

TRIBO

NEDUU

RONCEE

BLARPU

Stick by me.

I'm getting soaked.

WHEN IT STARTED TO RAIN HARD DURING THE BASEBALL GAME, THE FANS ----

Now arrange the circled letters to form the surprise answer, as suggested by the above cartoon.

Print answer here

JUMBLE®

Unscramble these four Jumbles, one letter to each square, to form four ordinary words.

TRETU

PRIEW

RAREBB

AICEPE

What are you watching?

This lamb keeps chasing his mother. It is so cute!

I ♥ JUMBLE

THEY WATCHED THE VIDEO FEATURING THE FEMALE SHEEP ON ----

Now arrange the circled letters to form the surprise answer, as suggested by the above cartoon.

Print answer here " ◯◯◯ " - ◯◯◯◯

JUMBLE®

Unscramble these four Jumbles, one letter to each square, to form four ordinary words.

FUTSF

SIDYA

VIRATI

NEKLEN

What happened?

I don't know.

Well, everything looks good. We're not sure why you blacked out.

THEY COULDN'T FIGURE OUT WHY THE WOMAN HAD PASSED OUT ... THEY DIDN'T HAVE THE ----

Now arrange the circled letters to form the surprise answer, as suggested by the above cartoon.

Print answer here

JUMBLE®

Unscramble these four Jumbles, one letter
to each square, to form four ordinary words.

BALCE

SUFYS

GUTNEG

ATOOPT

I've checked everywhere. There's no sign of it.

I can't find it, either. This is not good.

TRYING TO FIND THEIR
MISPLACED MAP
WAS A ----

Now arrange the circled letters to form
the surprise answer, as suggested by the
above cartoon.

Print answer here

JUMBLE®

Unscramble these four Jumbles, one letter
to each square, to form four ordinary words.

SQUTE

CLUGH

CUDINT

LIYZLA

AFTER A LONG DAY, THE
TELEMARKETER WAS
READY TO ---

Now arrange the circled letters to form
the surprise answer, as suggested by the
above cartoon.

Print answer here

JUMBLE®

Unscramble these four Jumbles, one letter
to each square, to form four ordinary words.

FUINY

CRIPE

HSTIGT

UTELOT

This makes you
our highest paid
model.

I'll have to
invest most
of this for
retirement.

AFTER SIGNING A HUGE
CONTRACT, THE FASHION
MODEL WAS ----

Now arrange the circled letters to form
the surprise answer, as suggested by the
above cartoon.

Print
answer
here

JUMBLE

Unscramble these four Jumbles, one letter to each square, to form four ordinary words.

FUNTI

GRRIO

WAGSEE

NITONO

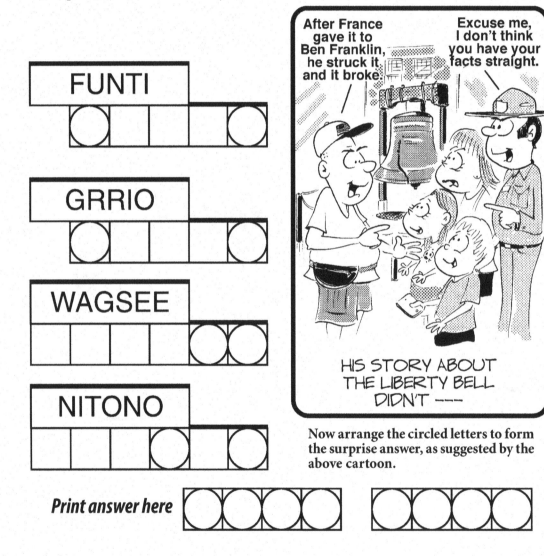

After France gave it to Ben Franklin, he struck it, and it broke.

Excuse me, I don't think you have your facts straight.

HIS STORY ABOUT THE LIBERTY BELL DIDN'T ----

Now arrange the circled letters to form the surprise answer, as suggested by the above cartoon.

Print answer here

JUMBLE®

Unscramble these four Jumbles, one letter to each square, to form four ordinary words.

CABKA

GODDE

GUTHHO

GREETR

I knew something was funny when he bought 5 tires.

Well, Mrs. Nussbaum, you have the right to remain silent...

For what?

AFTER TRYING TO USE A STOLEN CREDIT CARD, THE IDENTITY THIEF WAS GOING TO BE ----

Now arrange the circled letters to form the surprise answer, as suggested by the above cartoon.

Print answer here

JUMBLE®

Unscramble these four Jumbles, one letter
to each square, to form four ordinary words.

PREIV

KEOVE

TRSITH

SURIDA

My game has really improved here.

You two are up next.

You need to stop acing me.

THE TENNIS COURTS AT
THE MINIMUM SECURITY
PRISON FEATURED ----

Now arrange the circled letters to form
the surprise answer, as suggested by the
above cartoon.

Print answer here

JUMBLE®

Unscramble these four Jumbles, one letter
to each square, to form four ordinary words.

KIREH

BLIMC

DANTTE

VILASH

But you can't leave. You've been with us so long. You're the best.

I'm done. You can have my supplies. I won't need them anymore.

WHEN SHE QUIT HER JOB AS A HOUSEKEEPER, SHE MADE A ---

Now arrange the circled letters to form
the surprise answer, as suggested by the
above cartoon.

Print answer here

JUMBLE®

Unscramble these four Jumbles, one letter to each square, to form four ordinary words.

NEPDU

ROHAD

ZETALO

BOIMEZ

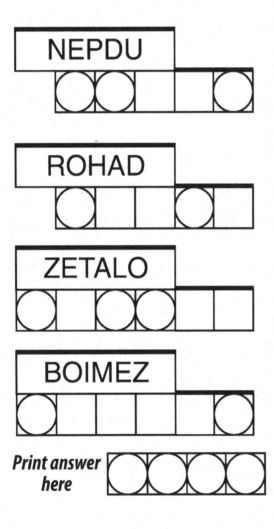

WHEN THEY CARVED THE JUMBLE INTO THE SIDE OF THE MOUNTAIN, THEY MADE A ---

Now arrange the circled letters to form the surprise answer, as suggested by the above cartoon.

Print answer here ☐☐☐☐

JUMBLE

Unscramble these four Jumbles, one letter
to each square, to form four ordinary words.

UNEEV

CLEIR

OLWOLF

POIUAT

Do you need to wind a rubber band to get that going?

Very funny. I can go 0-60 in 6 seconds and travel 200 miles on this charge.

LEAVING HIS ELECTRIC CAR PLUGGED IN ALL NIGHT MADE IT ---

Now arrange the circled letters to form
the surprise answer, as suggested by the
above cartoon.

Print answer "◯◯◯◯◯-◯◯◯◯"
here

JUMBLE®

Unscramble these four Jumbles, one letter
to each square, to form four ordinary words.

ACLNA

AVERB

MUTTOS

NINETT

What happened!
How could HE
knock YOU out?

I don't
have a
clue.

WHEN ASKED HOW A
SMALLER OPPONENT
HAD PULVERIZED HIM,
THE BOXER SAID ———

Now arrange the circled letters to form
the surprise answer, as suggested by the
above cartoon.

Print answer here ⬡⬡⬡⬡⬡ ⬡⬡

JUMBLE®

Unscramble these four Jumbles, one letter to each square, to form four ordinary words.

FETTH

SHURE

ODYMEC

PSAYSB

Why are you going to bed so early?

I need my rest. I'm going clubbing tomorrow.

THE CYCLOPS WENT TO BED BECAUSE HE WANTED TO GET ---

Now arrange the circled letters to form the surprise answer, as suggested by the above cartoon.

Print answer here

JUMBLE®

Unscramble these four Jumbles, one letter to each square, to form four ordinary words.

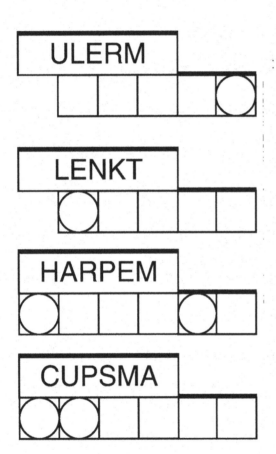

ULERM

LENKT

HARPEM

CUPSMA

Oh, my! That doesn't sound good. With you sitting in this damp basement, no wonder you're sick.

COUGH-COUGH-BLLLUUUUHH!!

JustJumble. com

THE COMPUTER PROGRAMMER WITH THE BAD COLD WAS A —--

Now arrange the circled letters to form the surprise answer, as suggested by the above cartoon.

Print answer here

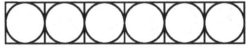

JUMBLE®

Unscramble these four Jumbles, one letter to each square, to form four ordinary words.

WUDEN

PRAAT

TALHEH

GUNHOE

I'm glad you're here. I can't play on this alone.

You can push me on the swings next.

WHEN THE TWINS WENT TO THE PARK TO PLAY, THEY WENT----

Now arrange the circled letters to form the surprise answer, as suggested by the above cartoon.

Print answer here "◯◯◯ - ◯◯◯◯◯◯◯"

JUMBLE®

Unscramble these four Jumbles, one letter to each square, to form four ordinary words.

MESUA

THOTO

HLLRIT

WELFAD

Where are you putting it all?

Keep it coming. I'm still hungry.

It's all-you-can-eat, right?

THEY WERE ENJOYING THE ALL-YOU-CAN-EAT STEAK RESTAURANT ----

Now arrange the circled letters to form the surprise answer, as suggested by the above cartoon.

Print answer here

50

JUMBLE®

Unscramble these four Jumbles, one letter
to each square, to form four ordinary words.

CHUNL

LHYIL

LAFUBI

TIPNUD

I can't believe this!
During a heat wave!
What is this going to
cost?

Honey,
you have
to cool
down.

This isn't
going to
be cheap.

AFTER THEIR AIR
CONDITIONER BROKE
DOWN AGAIN, SHE WISHED HER
HUSBAND COULD TAKE A ----

Now arrange the circled letters to form
the surprise answer, as suggested by the
above cartoon.

**Print answer
here**

JUMBLE®

Unscramble these four Jumbles, one letter
to each square, to form four ordinary words.

PREKO

NURKT

CEYNAG

POHNOC

Do you still
have the
"Eye of the
Tiger"?

Did you ever
get hurt
filming?

Yo,
Adrian!

SYLVESTER STALLONE
WANTED TO GO FOR A
RELAXING SWIM AT THE
BEACH, BUT IT WAS ----

Now arrange the circled letters to form
the surprise answer, as suggested by the
above cartoon.

Print answer here

JUMBLE®

Unscramble these four Jumbles, one letter to each square, to form four ordinary words.

TOXEL

HIDUM

RIFUGE

TYLLAF

WHAT THE WORKING MOM CONSIDERED HER EXERCISE HOUR.

Now arrange the circled letters to form the surprise answer, as suggested by the above cartoon.

Print answer here " ◯◯◯◯◯ " ◯◯◯◯◯

JUMBLE.

Unscramble these four Jumbles, one letter
to each square, to form four ordinary words.

TUDOO

REBBI

UNCIDE

EMBLUF

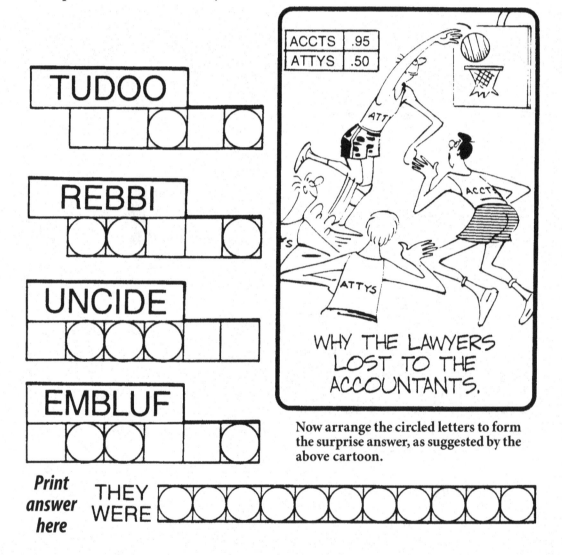

| ACCTS | .95 |
| ATTYS | .50 |

WHY THE LAWYERS
LOST TO THE
ACCOUNTANTS.

Now arrange the circled letters to form
the surprise answer, as suggested by the
above cartoon.

*Print
answer
here*

THEY
WERE

JUMBLE®

Unscramble these four Jumbles, one letter to each square, to form four ordinary words.

UNPER

CHOAR

SLICHE

CLAGEN

I'll take them

He'll win easily

WHAT HE WAS CONSIDERED IN THE SALES MARATHON.

Now arrange the circled letters to form the surprise answer, as suggested by the above cartoon.

Print answer here A ⬡⬡⬡⬡⬡ – ⬡⬡

JUMBLE®

Unscramble these four Jumbles, one letter
to each square, to form four ordinary words.

KELLN

GAADE

CORTER

BECKED

This is
gonna
cost you

WHAT HAPPENED TO
THE SAILOR WHO
MISSED HIS SHIP?

Now arrange the circled letters to form
the surprise answer, as suggested by the
above cartoon.

Print answer here HE
WAS " 〇〇〇〇〇〇 "

JUMBLE.

Unscramble these four Jumbles, one letter
to each square, to form four ordinary words.

VALEE

YAIRN

MAJEST

AVEGAS

It brings out
his personality

HOW THE PHOTO-
GRAPHER ACHIEVED
POSITIVE RESULTS.

Now arrange the circled letters to form
the surprise answer, as suggested by the
above cartoon.

Print answer here WITH

JUMBLE®

Unscramble these four Jumbles, one letter
to each square, to form four ordinary words.

BYDAN

DULGI

LARNAC

FICTEN

He pushed
all the
right
buttons

‒ *VICE PRESIDENT* ‒

THAT SNEAKY
ACCOUNTANT GOT
THE PROMOTION
BECAUSE HE WAS‒‒‒‒

Now arrange the circled letters to form
the surprise answer, as suggested by the
above cartoon.

Print answer "   "
here

JUMBLE®

Unscramble these four Jumbles, one letter
to each square, to form four ordinary words.

ENVOW

RORYS

CROSCH

DAUSIN

Phone

!#%!!!
Can't you
see I'm
busy?!

WHAT THE PUZZLE-
MAKER HAD FOR
HIS ASSISTANT.

Now arrange the circled letters to form
the surprise answer, as suggested by the
above cartoon.

Print answer here

JUMBLE®

Unscramble these four Jumbles, one letter
to each square, to form four ordinary words.

BUCCI

PRUPE

NITTEK

CAMENE

Beautiful!

Nothing
to it

WHAT THE GUESTS
CONSIDERED THE
BAKER'S MASTERPIECE.

Now arrange the circled letters to form
the surprise answer, as suggested by the
above cartoon.

Print answer here A ⬡⬡⬡⬡⬡ OF ⬡⬡⬡⬡

JUMBLE

Unscramble these four Jumbles, one letter to each square, to form four ordinary words.

RICHA

HOUGD

LICIAT

RUTUNE

He never misses

WHEN THE POOL PLAYER TOOK HIS TURN HE WAS----

Now arrange the circled letters to form the surprise answer, as suggested by the above cartoon.

Print answer here ⬡⬡⬡⬡⬡ ON ⬡⬡⬡

JUMBLE®

Unscramble these four Jumbles, one letter
to each square, to form four ordinary words.

KASHY

SYSMO

ABHORR

BOWELL

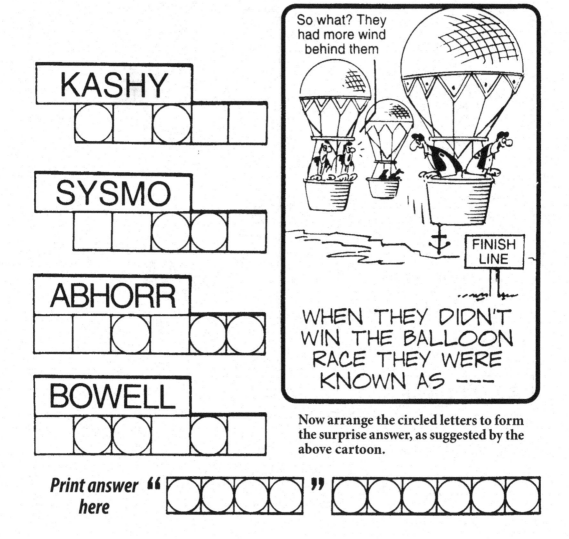

So what? They
had more wind
behind them

FINISH
LINE

WHEN THEY DIDN'T
WIN THE BALLOON
RACE THEY WERE
KNOWN AS ----

Now arrange the circled letters to form
the surprise answer, as suggested by the
above cartoon.

Print answer here " ⬡⬡⬡⬡ " ⬡⬡⬡⬡⬡⬡⬡

JUMBLE®

Unscramble these four Jumbles, one letter to each square, to form four ordinary words.

TOHRT

GEISE

THUNGA

KOVINE

'Till we meet again

WHAT KING ARTHUR'S GIRL SAID BEFORE THEY PARTED.

Now arrange the circled letters to form the surprise answer, as suggested by the above cartoon.

Print answer here

" ⬡⬡⬡⬡⬡⬡ , ⬡⬡⬡⬡⬡⬡⬡ "

JUMBLE®

Unscramble these four Jumbles, one letter to each square, to form four ordinary words.

VAIST

PIMBL

CAPMEN

EXFLAN

Isn't he a doll?

6-7

THEY ADORED THE HORN PLAYER BECAUSE HE HAD ----

Now arrange the circled letters to form the surprise answer, as suggested by the above cartoon.

Print answer here " ◯◯◯ ◯◯◯◯◯◯◯ "

JUMBLE

Unscramble these four Jumbles, one letter
to each square, to form four ordinary words.

HUBOG

RUHTT

COPILY

CUPSAM

Nice game, dear

WHAT THE COUPLE
CALLED THEIR
TENNIS DATES.

Now arrange the circled letters to form
the surprise answer, as suggested by the
above cartoon.

Print answer here A

JUMBLE®

Unscramble these four Jumbles, one letter
to each square, to form four ordinary words.

RYRUH

TOSOY

REFRET

DULSHO

Wasn't traffic terrible this morning!

EVERY morning!

WHAT LINEMEN CALL
THE MINUTES IN A
FOOTBALL GAME.

Now arrange the circled letters to form
the surprise answer, as suggested by the
above cartoon.

Print answer here "⬡⬡⬡⬡⬡" ⬡⬡⬡⬡

JUMBLE®

Unscramble these four Jumbles, one letter to each square, to form four ordinary words.

NEFTO

ZIPER

MOVULE

TUSHIA

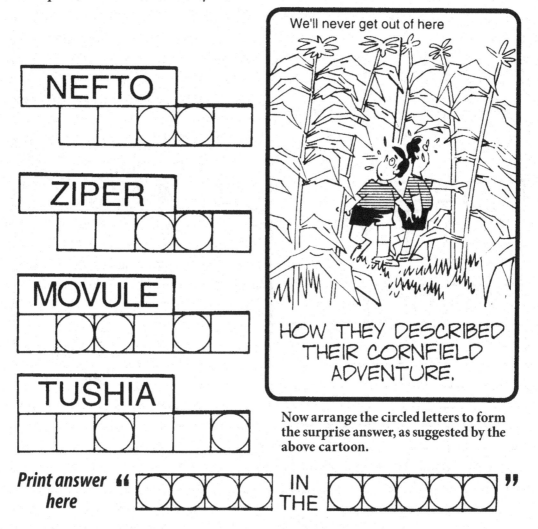

We'll never get out of here

HOW THEY DESCRIBED THEIR CORNFIELD ADVENTURE.

Now arrange the circled letters to form the surprise answer, as suggested by the above cartoon.

Print answer here " ◯◯◯◯ IN THE ◯◯◯◯◯ "

JUMBLE®

Unscramble these four Jumbles, one letter
to each square, to form four ordinary words.

NUGLE

SAREE

TANTIA

ZARLID

This is
getting serious

HOW THE
PASSERS-BY FOUND
THE DEMONSTRATION.

Now arrange the circled letters to form
the surprise answer, as suggested by the
above cartoon.

Print answer here

JUMBLE

Unscramble these four Jumbles, one letter
to each square, to form four ordinary words.

SUPEA

DEWUN

DHELVA

HEWPEN

It's back to Podunk for you

HOW THE PITCHER
FELT AFTER HE
WAS SENT TO
THE SHOWERS.

Now arrange the circled letters to form
the surprise answer, as suggested by the
above cartoon.

Print answer here ALL

JUMBLE®

Unscramble these four Jumbles, one letter
to each square, to form four ordinary words.

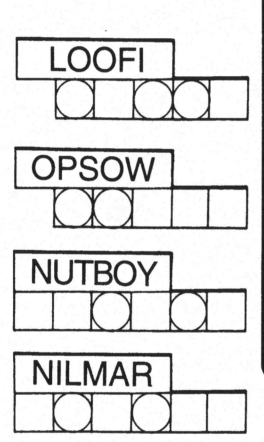

LOOFI

OPSOW

NUTBOY

NILMAR

That stupid diet doesn't work

WHEN YOU
CHEAT ON YOUR
DIET THE RESULT
CAN BE ----

Now arrange the circled letters to form
the surprise answer, as suggested by the
above cartoon.

Print answer " ◯◯◯◯◯ " – ◯◯◯◯◯
here

JUMBLE®

Unscramble these four Jumbles, one letter
to each square, to form four ordinary words.

DOORE

SATTY

MYPLOC

SNIDUM

How many
did we cut?

I
don't
know

HOW THE LOGGERS
LEFT THE FOREST.

Now arrange the circled letters to form
the surprise answer, as suggested by the
above cartoon.

Print answer here

71

JUMBLE®

Unscramble these four Jumbles, one letter
to each square, to form four ordinary words.

LAWRB

RAVAL

EDDOCE

REVOND

It's not moving

I want to go up

WHEN THE ELEVATOR
GOT STUCK,
IT WAS THIS.

Now arrange the circled letters to form
the surprise answer, as suggested by the
above cartoon.

Print answer here A " ◯◯◯◯◯◯◯ "

JUMBLE

Unscramble these four Jumbles, one letter
to each square, to form four ordinary words.

THOIS

SESMY

PORTHY

GUBLIN

This will pay for the footwear

ALOON

ONE WHO FORGES
—A COMMON NAME.

Now arrange the circled letters to form
the surprise answer, as suggested by the
above cartoon.

Print answer here ⬡⬡⬡⬡⬡

JUMBLE®

Unscramble these four Jumbles, one letter
to each square, to form four ordinary words.

LAKBY

MYLAN

GORCED

INZAIN

Mediterranean
Sea

FAMOUS MIDDLE
EAST "STRIP."

Now arrange the circled letters to form
the surprise answer, as suggested by the
above cartoon.

Print answer here

JUMBLE®

Unscramble these four Jumbles, one letter
to each square, to form four ordinary words.

YATHS

NARCH

KEETAB

CILIAT

My darling husband!

WHERE THE CHAMP'S
"PURSE" ENDED UP.

Now arrange the circled letters to form
the surprise answer, as suggested by the
above cartoon.

Print answer here

JUMBLE®

Unscramble these four Jumbles, one letter
to each square, to form four ordinary words.

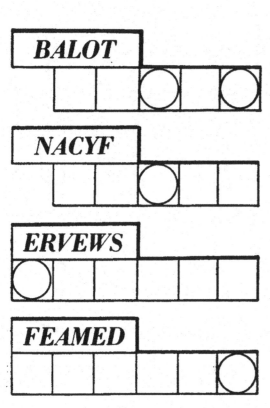

BALOT

NACYF

ERVEWS

FEAMED

THIS KIND OF
MONEY MIGHT COME
FROM A STONE.

Now arrange the circled letters to form
the surprise answer, as suggested by the
above cartoon.

Print answer here

JUMBLE®

Unscramble these four Jumbles, one letter
to each square, to form four ordinary words.

CUDEN

SHWIK

YORRAM

KORBEN

Guess we can't beat
him up today

WHAT TO WEAR
TO AVOID BLOWS.

Now arrange the circled letters to form
the surprise answer, as suggested by the
above cartoon.

Print answer here **A**

JUMBLE®

Unscramble these four Jumbles, one letter
to each square, to form four ordinary words.

CRAID

WECIN

KAJECT

DEMUGS

Why not a WORK
break for a change?

Thinks he's
smart

SOUNDS LIKE A
FUNNY BREAK.

Now arrange the circled letters to form
the surprise answer, as suggested by the
above cartoon.

Print answer here **A** "◯◯◯◯ ◯◯◯◯◯"

JUMBLE®

Unscramble these four Jumbles, one letter
to each square, to form four ordinary words.

LARVO

ZYZID

CHAPIL

LIGARC

Come here!

KEEP AWAY FROM
THIS EMPTY SPACE!

Now arrange the circled letters to form
the surprise answer, as suggested by the
above cartoon.

Print answer here "◯ - ◯◯◯◯"

JUMBLE®

Unscramble these four Jumbles, one letter
to each square, to form four ordinary words.

MONDE

BOJAN

TERVOX

NORMAT

Love those islands!

GO THERE IF YOU'RE CRAZY ABOUT IT!

Now arrange the circled letters to form
the surprise answer, as suggested by the
above cartoon.

Print answer here " ◯◯◯◯◯◯◯◯◯◯ "

JUMBLE®

Unscramble these four Jumbles, one letter
to each square, to form four ordinary words.

FEASH

LAMEY

SORABB

THRUNE

PUT ON SOME FAT!

Now arrange the circled letters to form
the surprise answer, as suggested by the
above cartoon.

Print answer here

JUMBLE®

Unscramble these four Jumbles, one letter
to each square, to form four ordinary words.

TACHY

YURST

LEEDUG

GLANJE

TRYING—IN A BOX.

Now arrange the circled letters to form
the surprise answer, as suggested by the
above cartoon.

Print answer here

JUMBLE®

Unscramble these four Jumbles, one letter to each square, to form four ordinary words.

IRQUE

LIENN

CILOPY

SHORUC

Yes, guv'nor

"E's just received a knight-hood

WHAT THEY CALLED THE BRITISH BEEF TYCOON.

Now arrange the circled letters to form the surprise answer, as suggested by the above cartoon.

Print answer here "☐☐☐ ☐☐☐☐"

JUMBLE®

Unscramble these four Jumbles, one letter
to each square, to form four ordinary words.

NORIM

PIMSK

THROXE

SIGAHR

WHAT A SEAL
MIGHT MAKE,

Now arrange the circled letters to form
the surprise answer, as suggested by the
above cartoon.

Print answer here **AN** ◯◯◯◯◯◯◯◯◯◯

JUMBLE®

Unscramble these four Jumbles, one letter
to each square, to form four ordinary words.

EEDUL

TARFD

PENOLL

RODAFE

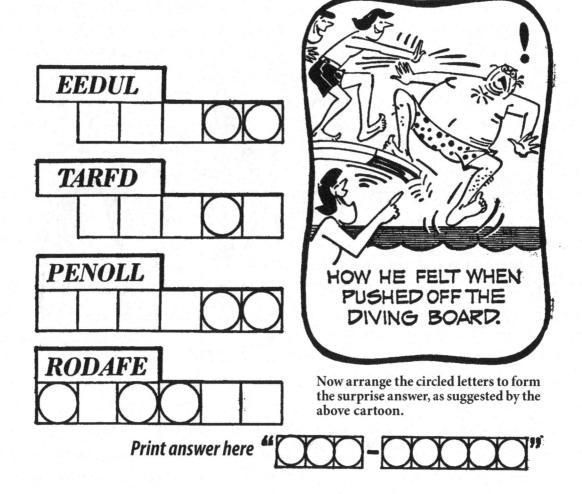

HOW HE FELT WHEN
PUSHED OFF THE
DIVING BOARD.

Now arrange the circled letters to form
the surprise answer, as suggested by the
above cartoon.

Print answer here "◯◯◯ – ◯◯◯◯◯"

JUMBLE®

Unscramble these four Jumbles, one letter to each square, to form four ordinary words.

CLECY

GROOF

YITMID

INSOOP

I'm not that ancient!

♪ MINUETS ♪

WHAT THE QUARRELING MUSICIANS SETTLED.

Now arrange the circled letters to form the surprise answer, as suggested by the above cartoon.

Print answer here AN ☐☐☐☐ ☐☐☐☐☐☐

JUMBLE®

Unscramble these four Jumbles, one letter
to each square, to form four ordinary words.

FOBEG

NILTE

CUPHIC

QUORIL

Ugh! Fish!

IT'S QUITE A JOB—
LET THERE BE NO
BONES ABOUT IT!

Now arrange the circled letters to form
the surprise answer, as suggested by the
above cartoon.

Print answer here

JUMBLE®

Unscramble these four Jumbles, one letter
to each square, to form four ordinary words.

ROWCE

TALUF

ABDALL

GETMAN

WHAT YOU'RE APT TO FIND UP A POLICEMAN'S SLEEVE.

Now arrange the circled letters to form
the surprise answer, as suggested by the
above cartoon.

Print answer here **THE** ⬡⬡⬡ ⬡⬡ **THE** ⬡⬡⬡

JUMBLE.

Unscramble these four Jumbles, one letter
to each square, to form four ordinary words.

REVVE

PECOU

LEMITY

BENTON

I made
money in
Wall Street

I made
money in
real estate

I made
money
gambling

(Gulp)

LOSE IT AND
YOU'LL HAVE
NOTHING TO SAY.

Now arrange the circled letters to form
the surprise answer, as suggested by the
above cartoon.

Print answer here

JUMBLE®

Unscramble these four Jumbles, one letter to each square, to form four ordinary words.

BARIB

MUIBE

NOGALS

TREVIN

You'll never believe what got away!

TELL THEM WHEN NO ONE BELIEVES IT!

Now arrange the circled letters to form the surprise answer, as suggested by the above cartoon.

Print answer here THE ◯◯◯◯◯◯◯◯

JUMBLE®

Unscramble these four Jumbles, one letter
to each square, to form four ordinary words.

INGEF

LECEX

RATTAR

RELPHE

WHAT'S IN THIS
STANDS OUT.

Now arrange the circled letters to form
the surprise answer, as suggested by the
above cartoon.

Print answer here

JUMBLE®

Unscramble these four Jumbles, one letter
to each square, to form four ordinary words.

YOFAR

TULGI

DRYBAN

POMLEY

Hurry----get up
there and
scare off
the stragglers

BLASTING
AREA

5-16

FLIES TO
GIVE WARNING.

Now arrange the circled letters to form
the surprise answer, as suggested by the
above cartoon.

Print answer here A ⬡◯◯◯ ◯◯◯◯◯

92

JUMBLE®

Unscramble these four Jumbles, one letter
to each square, to form four ordinary words.

LEWNY

TEELI

RETANB

ENKASH

WHAT LIFE UNDER
CANVAS MIGHT BE.

Now arrange the circled letters to form
the surprise answer, as suggested by the
above cartoon.

Print answer here

93

JUMBLE®

Unscramble these four Jumbles, one letter
to each square, to form four ordinary words.

TOUHY

LOOFI

BLUEBB

STEEWF

A PARTY WHERE
SOME GUESTS MIGHT
BE EXTINGUISHED.

Now arrange the circled letters to form
the surprise answer, as suggested by the
above cartoon.

Print answer here **A** ☐☐☐☐☐☐☐☐

JUMBLE®

Unscramble these four Jumbles, one letter
to each square, to form four ordinary words.

HYSIF

ELLAP

PAFFOY

LEMDEY

Big
shot!

HAS A PROMINENT
POSITION IN
THE COUNTRY.

Now arrange the circled letters to form
the surprise answer, as suggested by the
above cartoon.

Print answer here

JUMBLE®

Unscramble these four Jumbles, one letter
to each square, to form four ordinary words.

REHKI

PROOD

BELNAG

NAHVIS

Saved
expenses

WHY IT'S CHEAPER
TO EAT OUT
OF DOORS.

Now arrange the circled letters to form
the surprise answer, as suggested by the
above cartoon.

Print answer here

JUMBLE®

Unscramble these four Jumbles, one letter to each square, to form four ordinary words.

TOHOB

ECKER

SMOTED

UNTEAB

Stole candy from a baby!

Ice only

IT'S **HARD** TO GET AS LOW AS THIS.

Now arrange the circled letters to form the surprise answer, as suggested by the above cartoon.

Print answer here

JUMBLE®

Unscramble these four Jumbles, one letter to each square, to form four ordinary words.

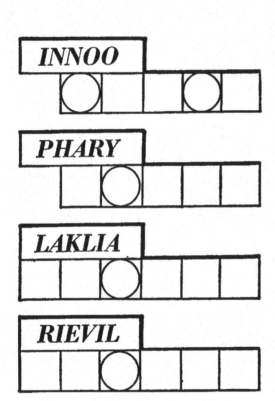

INNOO

PHARY

LAKLIA

RIEVIL

I've been swindled!

TWEET! TWEET!

THIS BIRD CHEATS AT CARDS.

Now arrange the circled letters to form the surprise answer, as suggested by the above cartoon.

Print answer here

JUMBLE®

Unscramble these four Jumbles, one letter
to each square, to form four ordinary words.

GEGAU

BEDIP

GOAUNT

DILANI

COULD BE THE
SUBJECT OF A
TENDER ATTACHMENT.

Now arrange the circled letters to form
the surprise answer, as suggested by the
above cartoon.

Print answer here **AN** ⬡⬡⬡⬡⬡⬡

JUMBLE®

Unscramble these four Jumbles, one letter
to each square, to form four ordinary words.

CAUTE

DEKEY

DILQUI

TORFOG

Take all your clothes off

Physical exam room

They've ruined me!

STRIPPED - IN A
SHEEPISH WAY.

Now arrange the circled letters to form
the surprise answer, as suggested by the
above cartoon.

Print answer here 〔 ◯◯◯◯◯◯◯ 〕

JUMBLE®

Unscramble these four Jumbles, one letter to each square, to form four ordinary words.

DEGIM

ZAUGE

HERZIT

GIRONI

LECTURE TONIGHT:
"How to Cut Down..."

A COURSE·TAKEN
BY PEOPLE WHO
OVERDO IT.

Now arrange the circled letters to form the surprise answer, as suggested by the above cartoon.

Print answer here ◯◯◯◯◯◯

JUMBLE

Unscramble these four Jumbles, one letter
to each square, to form four ordinary words.

ULIGE

BUNGE

MODDEO

CIRPAY

Just a little
bit on top

Now arrange the circled letters to form
the surprise answer, as suggested by the
above cartoon.

Print answer here " ◯◯◯◯◯ ◯◯◯◯ "

JUMBLE®

Unscramble these four Jumbles, one letter
to each square, to form four ordinary words.

EAPEY

HOOTT

SERVTY

FYLLAT

Never had
a chance!

OBVIOUSLY NOT RIGHT
FROM THE START..

Now arrange the circled letters to form
the surprise answer, as suggested by the
above cartoon.

Print answer
here ☐☐☐☐ ☐☐ **THE** ☐☐☐☐

JUMBLE.

Unscramble these four Jumbles, one letter
to each square, to form four ordinary words.

GUJED

NYMAG

CEEDOD

MINTIG

OLD-FASHIONED BUT
SEEMS TO HAVE PLENTY
OF BOYFRIENDS.

Now arrange the circled letters to form
the surprise answer, as suggested by the
above cartoon.

Print answer here "  "

JUMBLE®

Unscramble these four Jumbles, one letter
to each square, to form four ordinary words.

CANKK

POUMI

TRYSAP

VOCENX

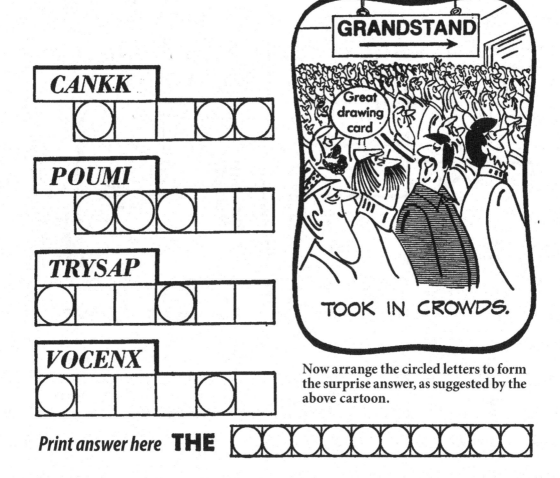

GRANDSTAND →

Great
drawing
card

TOOK IN CROWDS.

Now arrange the circled letters to form
the surprise answer, as suggested by the
above cartoon.

Print answer here **THE** ⬡⬡⬡⬡⬡⬡⬡⬡⬡⬡⬡⬡

JUMBLE®

Unscramble these four Jumbles, one letter
to each square, to form four ordinary words.

GLIBE

KLUSK

YAXTIL

MORTER

Holds on to
his job

He'll never
advance

Too
quiet

KEEP IT AND
YOU WON'T MOVE!

Now arrange the circled letters to form
the surprise answer, as suggested by the
above cartoon.

Print answer here

JUMBLE®

Unscramble these four Jumbles, one letter
to each square, to form four ordinary words.

OYLED

SOYUM

REHAWL

TURTEG

THEY SOUND CATTY.

Now arrange the circled letters to form
the surprise answer, as suggested by the
above cartoon.

Print answer here "⬡⬡⬡⬡⬡"

JUMBLE®

Unscramble these four Jumbles, one letter
to each square, to form four ordinary words.

NUMIS

REWFE

WHAREK

BIMBIE

Best sermon I think
I've ever heard!

A CONCLUSION
ONE MIGHT
MAKE AT CHURCH.

Now arrange the circled letters to form
the surprise answer, as suggested by the
above cartoon.

Print answer here " ◯◯◯◯ "

JUMBLE®

Unscramble these four Jumbles, one letter
to each square, to form four ordinary words.

NUMOR

LEDIY

SESAUR

ROYSAR

Some helper!

WHERE TO LOOK FOR
A HELPING HAND.

Now arrange the circled letters to form
the surprise answer, as suggested by the
above cartoon.

Print
answer
here

THE ◯◯◯ **OF** ◯◯◯◯◯ ◯◯◯

JUMBLE.

Unscramble these four Jumbles, one letter
to each square, to form four ordinary words.

NICCY

MOVEN

YERRAT

PICOMY

For you

Two more drafts!

WHEN THE BARTENDER'S
AWAY THERE SHOULD
BE ANOTHER...

Now arrange the circled letters to form
the surprise answer, as suggested by the
above cartoon.

Print answer here ◯◯ ◯◯◯

JUMBLE®

Unscramble these four Jumbles, one letter to each square, to form four ordinary words.

BELZA

UNMOD

ACDAFE

YAUNES

HOW THE LOSER RAN.

3-24

Now arrange the circled letters to form the surprise answer, as suggested by the above cartoon.

Print answer here "☐☐☐☐"

JUMBLE®

Unscramble these four Jumbles, one letter
to each square, to form four ordinary words.

GNUST

EXOID

RUCCIS

KESNIC

TEN SONS MIGHT COMPOSE THESE POEMS.

Now arrange the circled letters to form
the surprise answer, as suggested by the
above cartoon.

Print answer here " "

JUMBLE®

Unscramble these four Jumbles, one letter to each square, to form four ordinary words.

TUMON

MOAXI

EMTYSS

LERCEY

How shall I begin?

I'll get to the bottom of this!

MAY BE USED AS AN OPENING FOR A LETTER.

Now arrange the circled letters to form the surprise answer, as suggested by the above cartoon.

Print answer here ◯◯◯◯◯

113

JUMBLE®

**Unscramble these four Jumbles, one letter
to each square, to form four ordinary words.**

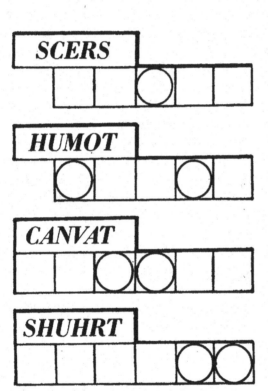

SCERS

HUMOT

CANVAT

SHUHRT

Dare I?

M. D.

COOKING

**MANY PEOPLE TEAR
'EM OUT OF BOOKS.**

Now arrange the circled letters to form
the surprise answer, as suggested by the
above cartoon.

Print answer here

JUMBLE®

Unscramble these four Jumbles, one letter
to each square, to form four ordinary words.

TUFON

PRUSN

UPLEDD

DACROW

EXPRESS

WHY HE COULDN'T GET
OFF THE BUS.

Now arrange the circled letters to form
the surprise answer, as suggested by the
above cartoon.

Print answer here **IT WAS** "⬡⬡⬡⬡⬡⬡⬡"

JUMBLE®

Unscramble these four Jumbles, one letter to each square, to form four ordinary words.

METOC

SURVI

YUTPED

REATEA

WHAT ONE SHOT
SOMETIMES STARTS.

Now arrange the circled letters to form the surprise answer, as suggested by the above cartoon.

Print answer here

JUMBLE®

Unscramble these four Jumbles, one letter
to each square, to form four ordinary words.

SYNIH

LOVEC

NAKTIE

RERROT

Wild

NO VEINS IN THIS
KIND OF MEAT.

Now arrange the circled letters to form
the surprise answer, as suggested by the
above cartoon.

Print answer here

JUMBLE®

Unscramble these four Jumbles, one letter
to each square, to form four ordinary words.

RAHME

GERME

DELIRB

SPOOPE

See? Nothing to it!

IT'S NOT DIFFICULT TO DO THINGS WITH IT.

3-16

Now arrange the circled letters to form
the surprise answer, as suggested by the
above cartoon.

Print answer here ⬡⬡⬡⬡

118

JUMBLE®

Unscramble these four Jumbles, one letter
to each square, to form four ordinary words.

ROCKA

TOINX

GELISH

BRUETT

Play something classical!

HE LEFT ME AN' I'M SA-A-A-A-D

SOUNDS LIKE
LIGHT MUSIC.

Now arrange the circled letters to form
the surprise answer, as suggested by the
above cartoon.

Print answer here **A** ⬡⬡⬡⬡⬡ ⬡⬡⬡⬡

JUMBLE®

Unscramble these four Jumbles, one letter
to each square, to form four ordinary words.

VICLI

DARUG

HUCHAN

GEDDUR

I can lick any dame
in the house!

HER CAPACITY
IS 8 PINTS.

Now arrange the circled letters to form
the surprise answer, as suggested by the
above cartoon.

Print answer here

JUMBLE®

Unscramble these four Jumbles, one letter to each square, to form four ordinary words.

ROBOK

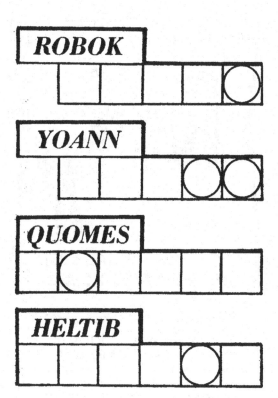

YOANN

QUOMES

HELTIB

SOMETIMES PLAYED IN ONE'S ABSENCE.

Now arrange the circled letters to form the surprise answer, as suggested by the above cartoon.

Print answer here

JUMBLE®

Unscramble these four Jumbles, one letter
to each square, to form four ordinary words.

SHLYP

INGIC

TOYBUN

DRAUWP

Psst!
Not
now!

PAYS AN INFORMAL VISIT
WHEN DAD'S HOME.

Now arrange the circled letters to form
the surprise answer, as suggested by the
above cartoon.

Print answer here

JUMBLE®

Unscramble these four Jumbles, one letter
to each square, to form four ordinary words.

VOPER

WEDIP

ANTOYB

UNRICH

PRANCED AROUND WITH
A RED CAPE.

Now arrange the circled letters to form
the surprise answer, as suggested by the
above cartoon.

Print answer here " ◯◯◯◯ - ◯◯◯ "

JUMBLE®

Unscramble these four Jumbles, one letter
to each square, to form four ordinary words.

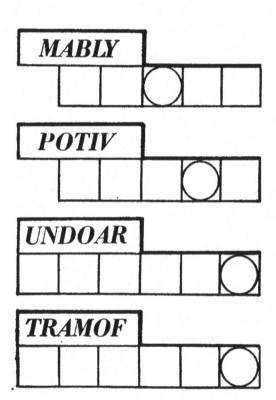

MABLY

POTIV

UNDOAR

TRAMOF

She knows how much I make

NOT KEPT IN THE DARK.

Now arrange the circled letters to form
the surprise answer, as suggested by the
above cartoon.

Print answer here "◯◯◯◯"

JUMBLE®

Unscramble these four Jumbles, one letter
to each square, to form four ordinary words.

RUPEN

LAAVI

TUNBOT

ELLAHT

FOLD IN CLOTH.

Now arrange the circled letters to form
the surprise answer, as suggested by the
above cartoon.

Print answer here

JUMBLE®

Unscramble these four Jumbles, one letter
to each square, to form four ordinary words.

CLIUD

TEGOB

LIVONI

SAYMUL

Take notes

IT'S NOT CLEAR WHAT'S
BEEN WRITTEN...

Now arrange the circled letters to form
the surprise answer, as suggested by the
above cartoon.

Print answer here

JUMBLE®

Unscramble these four Jumbles, one letter
to each square, to form four ordinary words.

TOJUS

GANTY

RETULB

NEWECH

THEY HELP TO KEEP
THE TENT UP.

Now arrange the circled letters to form
the surprise answer, as suggested by the
above cartoon.

Print answer here ◯◯◯ " ◯◯◯◯ "

JUMBLE®

Unscramble these four Jumbles, one letter
to each square, to form four ordinary words.

RILLT

SUPIO

BOILID

LEESAW

Sick
friend . . .

WHAT YOU MIGHT DO
OVER THE EYES.

Now arrange the circled letters to form
the surprise answer, as suggested by the
above cartoon.

Print answer here

128

JUMBLE®

Unscramble these four Jumbles, one letter to each square, to form four ordinary words.

CONOR

NARPO

RAUPPE

LIBART

Just waking up, dear?

AH—fit for the gods!

WHAT TO DRINK COMING OUT OF A TRANCE.

Now arrange the circled letters to form the surprise answer, as suggested by the above cartoon.

Print answer here [⟨ ⟩⟨ ⟩⟨ ⟩⟨ ⟩⟨ ⟩⟨ ⟩]

JUMBLE®

Unscramble these four Jumbles, one letter
to each square, to form four ordinary words.

MYLOD

ARROD

POLUCE

OLDBOY

Huh! A knight in shining armor!

Immature!

THIS DASHING YOUNG
MAN IS A MERE
BOY INSIDE!

Now arrange the circled letters to form
the surprise answer, as suggested by the
above cartoon.

Print answer here **A** " ◯ - ◯◯◯ - ◯ "

JUMBLE®

Unscramble these four Jumbles, one letter
to each square, to form four ordinary words.

HIRMT

AUZER

SNEEWT

MAJEST

STOP- THEN CHARGE!

Now arrange the circled letters to form
the surprise answer, as suggested by the
above cartoon.

Print answer here ⬡⬡⬡⬡⬡⬡

JUMBLE®

Unscramble these four Jumbles, one letter
to each square, to form four ordinary words.

LEROD

ZYCAR

VELMAR

GOCHUR

Once upon a time . . .

LONG AGO THERE
WERE DAYS OF IT.

Now arrange the circled letters to form
the surprise answer, as suggested by the
above cartoon.

Print answer here "ⵔⵔⵔⵔ"

132

JUMBLE®

Unscramble these four Jumbles, one letter
to each square, to form four ordinary words.

DUPON

MOWNE

CHUNQE

KLAYEC

WHERE A WAITER
MIGHT FIND A
GOOD TIP.

Now arrange the circled letters to form
the surprise answer, as suggested by the
above cartoon.

Print answer here ⬡⬡ **A** ⬡⬡⬡ ⬡⬡⬡

JUMBLE®

Unscramble these four Jumbles, one letter
to each square, to form four ordinary words.

LEKAN

KNARC

ENFADE

MILTEG

MAGIC SHOW

STAGE DOOR

WHERE TO GO IN AND
CAST A SPELL.

Now arrange the circled letters to form
the surprise answer, as suggested by the
above cartoon.

Print answer here " ◯◯◯◯◯◯◯◯ "

JUMBLE®

Unscramble these four Jumbles, one letter
to each square, to form four ordinary words.

PLIME

GORAC

STEFIA

TENNIT

MORE AGREEABLE—
WITH ICE IN IT!

Now arrange the circled letters to form
the surprise answer, as suggested by the
above cartoon.

Print answer here " ☐ - ☐☐☐ - ☐ "

JUMBLE®

Unscramble these four Jumbles, one letter
to each square, to form four ordinary words.

WEPOR

PAPYL

MANCEP

YILSAM

BEDDING

— Try it

SHOWS WHAT THE REST
OUGHT TO BE LIKE.

Now arrange the circled letters to form
the surprise answer, as suggested by the
above cartoon.

Print answer here **A**

136

JUMBLE®

Unscramble these four Jumbles, one letter
to each square, to form four ordinary words.

TENGA

KREAM

LANTUF

POSHIN

The boat's back!

FERRY SCHEDULE

Now arrange the circled letters to form
the surprise answer, as suggested by the
above cartoon.

Print answer here " ◯◯◯◯◯ "

JUMBLE®

Unscramble these four Jumbles, one letter
to each square, to form four ordinary words.

OCKAL

GEALL

LEYRAR

FLIECK

MIGHT RING HIS NECK!

Now arrange the circled letters to form
the surprise answer, as suggested by the
above cartoon.

Print answer here

JUMBLE®

Unscramble these four Jumbles, one letter
to each square, to form four ordinary words.

ICMEN

DUESE

PONGIE

CROAFT

THEY MAY GIVE
YOU IDEAS.

Now arrange the circled letters to form
the surprise answer, as suggested by the
above cartoon.

Print answer here

JUMBLE®

Unscramble these four Jumbles, one letter
to each square, to form four ordinary words.

ENFLO

RIGMY

TUEBAY

LOGYOM

Charge
or cash?

Behave—I'm spending
plenty on you

SOMETIMES TAKEN
OUT SHOPPING—
BUT NOT ALWAYS.

Now arrange the circled letters to form
the surprise answer, as suggested by the
above cartoon.

Print answer here ◯◯◯◯◯

JUMBLE®

Unscramble these four Jumbles, one letter to each square, to form four ordinary words.

ACOME

POSOT

THINGK

MEALEN

Pay you back tomorrow

Don't believe it

WHEN MIGHT HE KEEP HIS WORD?

Now arrange the circled letters to form the surprise answer, as suggested by the above cartoon.

Print answer here

WHEN ☐☐ ☐☐☐ ☐☐☐☐☐ IT

JUMBLE®

Unscramble these four Jumbles, one letter
to each square, to form four ordinary words.

NEEYM

POANI

ENCOSH

JURINE

THESE STORIES ONLY
SOUND LIKE THEY'RE
SLOW-MOVING.

Now arrange the circled letters to form
the surprise answer, as suggested by the
above cartoon.

Print answer here ◯◯◯◯◯◯ ◯◯◯◯

JUMBLE®

Unscramble these four Jumbles, one letter
to each square, to form four ordinary words.

YOHNP

JOMAR

ACRIVA

BLUMFE

You're not going anywhere tonight

THIS BIRD WON'T STEAL OUT.

Now arrange the circled letters to form
the surprise answer, as suggested by the
above cartoon.

Print answer here A " ◯◯◯ - ◯◯ "

JUMBLE®

Unscramble these four Jumbles, one letter
to each square, to form four ordinary words.

HARCO

IMCAG

ZEEMAC

NIPICC

Forceful!

STRAIGHT FROM
THE SHOULDER!

Now arrange the circled letters to form
the surprise answer, as suggested by the
above cartoon.

Print answer here

JUMBLE®

Unscramble these four Jumbles, one letter
to each square, to form four ordinary words.

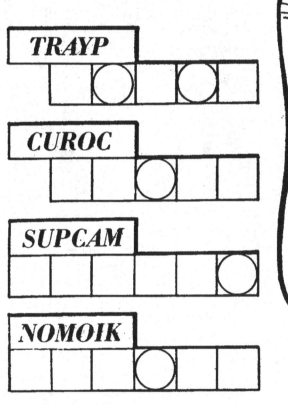

TRAYP

CUROC

SUPCAM

NOMOIK

YOU MIGHT CHANGE COATS FOR THIS OPERA!

Now arrange the circled letters to form
the surprise answer, as suggested by the
above cartoon.

Print answer here " ⬡⬡⬡⬡⬡ "

JUMBLE®

Unscramble these four Jumbles, one letter
to each square, to form four ordinary words.

DIGUL

NELOB

WARROM

NOIMOD

A tip!

A TOUCHING
REMINDER.

Now arrange the circled letters to form
the surprise answer, as suggested by the
above cartoon.

Print answer here

JUMBLE®

Unscramble these four Jumbles, one letter
to each square, to form four ordinary words.

VAYEH

LUFOR

SWEDIT

TINNEY

I say, Watson!

WHY THE BIGGEST
ANIMAL LEAVES
NO FOOTPRINTS.

Now arrange the circled letters to form
the surprise answer, as suggested by the
above cartoon.

*Print
answer
here* **THE** ☐☐☐☐☐☐ **HAS** ☐☐ ☐☐☐☐☐

JUMBLE®

Unscramble these four Jumbles, one letter to each square, to form four ordinary words.

TYREN

AKQUE

KRUTEY

SESCUN

YAK YAK YAK
YAK YAK YAK

In short—sit down!

Now arrange the circled letters to form the surprise answer, as suggested by the above cartoon.

Print answer here " ⬡⬡⬡⬡⬡ "

JUMBLE®

Unscramble these four Jumbles, one letter
to each square, to form four ordinary words.

LINAF

MAARD

WAMIDY

DEXOUS

MUST BE TAKEN
IN WATER.

Now arrange the circled letters to form
the surprise answer, as suggested by the
above cartoon.

Print answer here ◯ ◯◯◯◯

JUMBLE®

Unscramble these four Jumbles, one letter
to each square, to form four ordinary words.

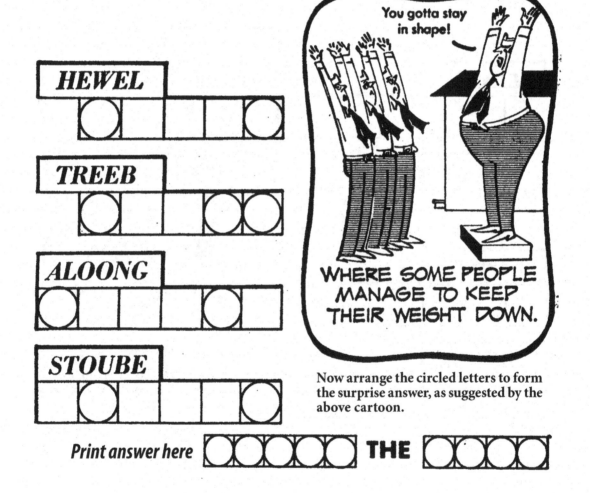

You gotta stay
in shape!

WHERE SOME PEOPLE
MANAGE TO KEEP
THEIR WEIGHT DOWN.

HEWEL

TREEB

ALOONG

STOUBE

Now arrange the circled letters to form
the surprise answer, as suggested by the
above cartoon.

Print answer here ◯◯◯◯◯ **THE** ◯◯◯◯

JUMBLE®

Unscramble these four Jumbles, one letter
to each square, to form four ordinary words.

VELED

CLAWR

WAYELE

LEEXAH

EXAM RESULTS

We both passed!

ONE MIGHT BE
RELIEVED TO SAY IT!

Now arrange the circled letters to form
the surprise answer, as suggested by the
above cartoon.

Print answer here " ◯◯◯◯ "

JUMBLE®

Unscramble these four Jumbles, one letter
to each square, to form four ordinary words.

THAWE

ESTAC

PHEPOR

YAWNAY

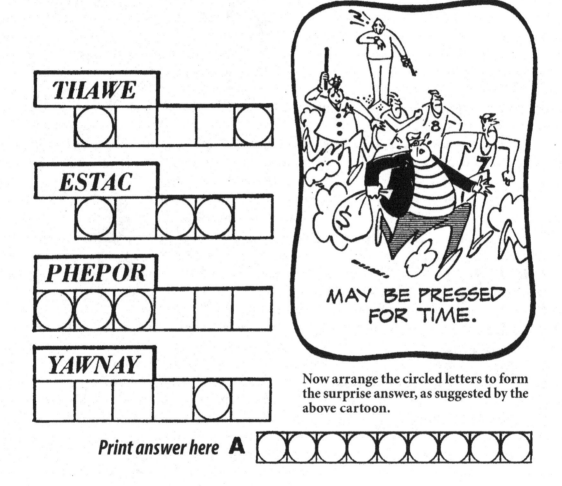

MAY BE PRESSED
FOR TIME.

Now arrange the circled letters to form
the surprise answer, as suggested by the
above cartoon.

Print answer here A

JUMBLE®

Unscramble these four Jumbles, one letter
to each square, to form four ordinary words.

FRIGE

YONIS

SAMOUF

JICTEN

How barbaric!

HOW ODD THAT IT
MIGHT BE SQUARE!

Now arrange the circled letters to form
the surprise answer, as suggested by the
above cartoon.

Print answer here ☐ ☐☐☐☐

JUMBLE®

Unscramble these four Jumbles, one letter
to each square, to form four ordinary words.

MALUB

ROSYR

INPROS

POITTE

Forever?

THIS COMPOSER
HAD AMERICA
RIGHT IN HIM!

Now arrange the circled letters to form
the surprise answer, as suggested by the
above cartoon.

Print answer here " ☐☐-☐. ☐. ☐. "

JUMBLE®

Unscramble these four Jumbles, one letter to each square, to form four ordinary words.

OEPLE

SELIA

ENSICC

DIPEEM

PUT DOWN TO COME UP.

Now arrange the circled letters to form the surprise answer, as suggested by the above cartoon.

Print answer here ⬡◯◯◯·◯◯

JUMBLE®

Unscramble these four Jumbles, one letter
to each square, to form four ordinary words.

KOSMY

RACHI

PECDIT

YEGLAC

ALL KINDS
OF DAIRY
PRODUCTS

THEY'D BE EXPECTED
TO LEAVE EGGS.

Now arrange the circled letters to form
the surprise answer, as suggested by the
above cartoon.

Print answer here

JUMBLE.

Unscramble these four Jumbles, one letter
to each square, to form four ordinary words.

AUPSE

ROVIY

NOYFLE

DRIMBO

YUM!

SMACK 'EM JUST FOR
PURE ENJOYMENT.

Now arrange the circled letters to form
the surprise answer, as suggested by the
above cartoon.

Print answer here

JUMBLE®

Unscramble these four Jumbles, one letter
to each square, to form four ordinary words.

VERAG

ANIFT

INREEM

LEEPPO

Congratulations!
All girls!

MATERNI

A PERSON WITHOUT
MALE OFFSPRING.

Now arrange the circled letters to form
the surprise answer, as suggested by the
above cartoon.

Print answer here " ⬡ ⬡⬡⬡ "

158

JUMBLE®

Unscramble these four Jumbles, one letter
to each square, to form four ordinary words.

NUCEL

IDLAY

JURNIY

MOOBBA

WORK OUT
AT THE
"Y"

A WELL-KNOWN
CLUB FOR GYMNASTS.

Now arrange the circled letters to form
the surprise answer, as suggested by the
above cartoon.

Print answer here **AN** ⬡⬡⬡⬡⬡⬡ ⬡⬡⬡⬡

JUMBLE®

Unscramble these four Jumbles, one letter
to each square, to form four ordinary words.

Shut the door quietly

THERE'S A CATCH
TO THIS ONE!

ALLIC

KICHT

B.ARKEY

FACTUE

Now arrange the circled letters to form
the surprise answer, as suggested by the
above cartoon.

Print answer here

JUMBLE®

Unscramble these four Jumbles, one letter
to each square, to form four ordinary words.

EPSIO

ROALS

DAMTLE

WHYTOR

WHAT THE PROVERBIAL
CARPENTER HAD
A COLLECTION OF.

Now arrange the circled letters to form
the surprise answer, as suggested by the
above cartoon.

Print answer here

JUMBLE®

Unscramble these four Jumbles, one letter
to each square, to form four ordinary words.

OUSLE

SESCH

PYTSHU

HOMARI

A PIECE OF
CHOPIN SUITABLE
AT DINNERTIME.

Now arrange the circled letters to form
the surprise answer, as suggested by the
above cartoon.

Print answer here " ◯◯◯◯ "

JUMBLE®

Theater

Challenger Puzzles

JUMBLE®

Unscramble these six Jumbles, one letter to each square, to form six ordinary words.

TORFUH

OZABEG

CUBASA

KAYWLE

NURADO

CEXTIO

We're so glad you came to visit!

We haven't seen you since you moved.

THE ZEBRAS STOPPED BY TO VISIT THE GIRAFFES WHEN THEY WERE IN THE GIRAFFES' ———

Now arrange the circled letters to form the surprise answer, as suggested by the above cartoon.

Print answer here

164

JUMBLE®

Unscramble these six Jumbles, one letter to each square, to form six ordinary words.

NNAILD

CFEETD

GLIHYH

KORECT

VERRFO

TAUDPE

The lift is operating so well!

I can't believe how smoothly the line is running!

THE SKI LIFT TO THE TOP OF THE MOUNTAIN WAS SO POPULAR BECAUSE OF ITS ---

Now arrange the circled letters to form the surprise answer, as suggested by the above cartoon.

Print answer here

JUMBLE®

Unscramble these six Jumbles, one letter to each square, to form six ordinary words.

CLEATK

GUNEHO

SYLAWA

AURPRO

CREWUF

MOICEN

Wow! They even have a farmer mascot here.

Look at that! They've thought of everything.

THE NEW GROCERY STORE WAS SO SUCCESSFUL THANKS TO ITS ----

Now arrange the circled letters to form the surprise answer, as suggested by the above cartoon.

Print answer here

JUMBLE®

Unscramble these six Jumbles, one letter to each square, to form six ordinary words.

LANHIE

SEROET

GISELH

KEYELM

CUGORH

RUTBAP

Since you're so interested in bones, you can stay after class and learn all of their names.

Like the head bone's attached to the neck bone?

He's so rude.

He's going to get it.

AFTER THE STUDENT DISRUPTED THE CLASS, THE TEACHER ———

Now arrange the circled letters to form the surprise answer, as suggested by the above cartoon.

Print answer here

JUMBLE®

Unscramble these six Jumbles, one letter to each square, to form six ordinary words.

TROYWH

CINTEE

PIESCT

MAIDYS

ATOANS

CIDTIN

What's that zombie doing?

He hasn't moved in an hour. I don't think I can save his life.

AHHHHH!

WHEN THE ZOMBIE WENT SWIMMING, HE WAS ----

Now arrange the circled letters to form the surprise answer, as suggested by the above cartoon.

Print answer here

168

JUMBLE®

Unscramble these six Jumbles, one letter
to each square, to form six ordinary words.

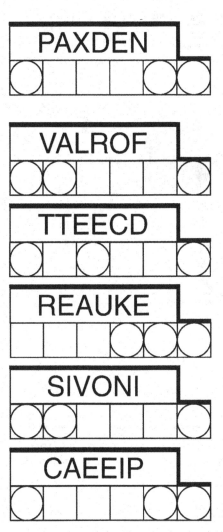

PAXDEN

VALROF

TTEECD

REAUKE

SIVONI

CAEEIP

How do you
like your
chances to
repeat here
at the
speedway?

All the cars are
running fast.
I'll have some
hurdles
to jump
in order
to win.

EVEN THOUGH IT'S A ROAD
RACE, THE INDIANAPOLIS 500
IS A —

Now arrange the circled letters to form
the surprise answer, as suggested by the
above cartoon.

Print answer here

169

JUMBLE®

Unscramble these six Jumbles, one letter to each square, to form six ordinary words.

TARMOL

PINNAK

TOEGAU

SHONEC

YETROH

SUMBAH

This is just my warm up lifting. Maybe you'd like to watch when I'm bench pressing.

The only thing you're pressing is your luck.

THE BODYBUILDER WASN'T GOING TO HAVE ANY LUCK WITH THE WOMAN BECAUSE HE ----

Now arrange the circled letters to form the surprise answer, as suggested by the above cartoon.

Print answer here

JUMBLE®

Unscramble these six Jumbles, one letter
to each square, to form six ordinary words.

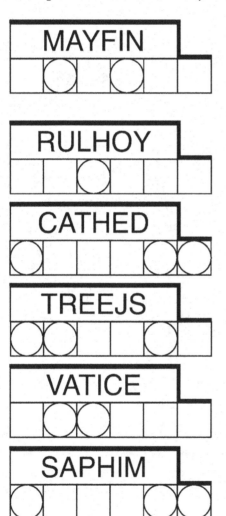

MAYFIN

RULHOY

CATHED

TREEJS

VATICE

SAPHIM

Would you
like to give
it a try?

You bet!
I've always wanted
to skydive!

GREAT
ALTITUDE
SKYDIVING
SCHOOL

ENTER TO
WIN A FREE
LESSON

WHEN HE SAW AN
OPPORTUNITY TO WIN
A FREE SKYDIVING
LESSON, HE ----

Now arrange the circled letters to form
the surprise answer, as suggested by the
above cartoon.

Print answer here

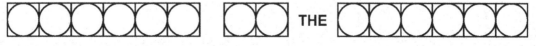

⬡⬡⬡⬡⬡⬡ ⬡⬡ THE ⬡⬡⬡⬡⬡⬡

JUMBLE®

Unscramble these six Jumbles, one letter to each square, to form six ordinary words.

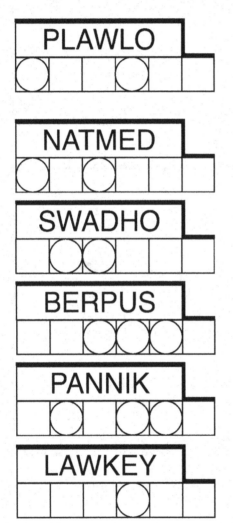

PLAWLO

NATMED

SWADHO

BERPUS

PANNIK

LAWKEY

Can you help us get to Old Faithful?

Sure. That's easy. I was headed that way. Follow me and I'll take you right to the geyser.

THE FOREST RANGER'S JOB WAS A ----

Now arrange the circled letters to form the surprise answer, as suggested by the above cartoon.

Print answer here

JUMBLE®

Unscramble these six Jumbles, one letter to each square, to form six ordinary words.

ATMOOT

DENOUN

EAGOIL

PURARO

POYBIS

LUCNOM

FINISH

Way to go, honey!

First place! I'll never forget this.

Smile.

FINISHING FIRST IN THE MARATHON CREATED A ---

Now arrange the circled letters to form the surprise answer, as suggested by the above cartoon.

Print answer here

JUMBLE®

Unscramble these six Jumbles, one letter to each square, to form six ordinary words.

AEDING

QUOMES

YATIRR

CRUSIC

YERRSH

HIRTED

HONK
HONK

STOP GO KNIGHTS! BEAT CENTRAL

HONK
HONK

WHEN THE SCHOOL
BAND GOT STUCK
IN TRAFFIC,
THEY ––

Now arrange the circled letters to form the surprise answer, as suggested by the above cartoon.

Print answer here

JUMBLE

Unscramble these six Jumbles, one letter to each square, to form six ordinary words.

NERUNG

SUTTRY

EPIDEM

DICHOR

PHISAR

FESTOF

This is on sale for $60

Over my limit

WHAT HE SAID WHEN HE BOUGHT THE $50 PERFUME.

Now arrange the circled letters to form the surprise answer, as suggested by the above cartoon.

Print answer here

◯◯◯ A " ◯◯◯◯◯ " ◯◯◯◯

JUMBLE.

Unscramble these six Jumbles, one letter to each square, to form six ordinary words.

FLOSSI

BAGLER

YEMINT

VINNET

LOMBIE

FEETOF

Grrrr

-!!@#

I'll knock your block off!

WHAT THE QUARTERBACK'S NASTY PASS PROTECTORS WERE KNOWN AS.

Now arrange the circled letters to form the surprise answer, as suggested by the above cartoon.

Print answer here

AN " ☐☐☐☐☐☐☐☐☐ " ☐☐☐☐

JUMBLE®

Unscramble these six Jumbles, one letter to each square, to form six ordinary words.

NAFELL

EVVELT

SHILER

ENCHEW

PERUPA

SERVTY

I feel so strange

What's wrong, Sara?

WHEN THE ACTRESS VISITED THE DOCTOR IN HER MOVIE ROLE, SHE ---

Now arrange the circled letters to form the surprise answer, as suggested by the above cartoon.

Print answer here

◯◯◯◯◯ ' ◯ " ◯◯◯◯◯◯◯◯ "

177

JUMBLE

Unscramble these six Jumbles, one letter to each square, to form six ordinary words.

SCOFIA

THUBOG

CHATED

TIPOLE

HOWDAS

KUEBER

Nobody is good enough for her

But, Matilda

WHEN MANY DIDN'T SUIT HER, SHE REMAINED ---

Now arrange the circled letters to form the surprise answer, as suggested by the above cartoon.

Print answer here

◯◯◯◯◯◯◯◯ A ◯◯◯◯◯◯◯

JUMBLE®

Unscramble these six Jumbles, one letter to each square, to form six ordinary words.

CLEPIN

NERBAN

NORBIN

SKABET

PERRIM

ANCIDD

WHY THE ENGINEER STAYED SINGULARLY FOCUSED ON HIS WORK.

Now arrange the circled letters to form the surprise answer, as suggested by the above cartoon.

Print answer here

HE HAD A ⬡⬡⬡ ⬡⬡⬡⬡⬡ ⬡⬡⬡⬡

JUMBLE®

Unscramble these six Jumbles, one letter to each square, to form six ordinary words.

PUNCOO

SPEEXO

NAUTER

RAYVOS

SOUREA

SERJEY

WHAT THE BUNGLING PHOTOGRAPHER GOT AT THE BEACH.

Now arrange the circled letters to form the surprise answer, as suggested by the above cartoon.

Print answer here

JUMBLE®

Unscramble these six Jumbles, one letter to each square, to form six ordinary words.

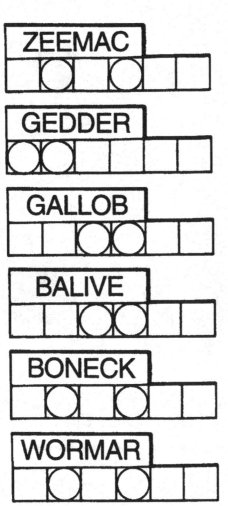

ZEEMAC

GEDDER

GALLOB

BALIVE

BONECK

WORMAR

HOW DID THE COWBOY BEAT THE HEAT?

Now arrange the circled letters to form the surprise answer, as suggested by the above cartoon.

Print answer here

HE

JUMBLE®

Unscramble these six Jumbles, one letter to each square, to form six ordinary words.

TRAINO

REDUME

LOONED

ZARABA

PLYENT

GAYMIB

GUARANTEED TO PUT
YOU TO SLEEP.

Now arrange the circled letters to form the surprise answer, as suggested by the above cartoon.

Print answer here

A " ◯◯◯◯◯◯ " ◯◯◯◯◯◯◯

JUMBLE

Unscramble these six Jumbles, one letter
to each square, to form six ordinary words.

BROWDY

DAGAPO

VELARM

EMBACE

DOLFYN

TASOAN

WHAT THE
BICYCLING
ENTREPRENEUR DID.

Now arrange the circled letters to form
the surprise answer, as suggested by the
above cartoon.

Print answer here

HE "◯◯◯◯◯◯◯◯" HIS ◯◯◯◯◯

Answers

1. **Jumbles:** HURRY SHRUG RELENT RANCID
   Answer: The cyclops couldn't help but notice the new arrival after she — CAUGHT HIS EYE

2. **Jumbles:** KHAKI ENACT AVENUE DUPLEX
   Answer: If Ichabod Crane was going to outrun Sleepy Hollow's horseman, he'd need to — KEEP AHEAD

3. **Jumbles:** WEAVE NINTH CUPFUL KNOTTY
   Answer: We couldn't come up with a new salad pun…If you have a good one — "LETTUCE" KNOW

4. **Jumbles:** CHAOS TOXIC MERELY KERNEL
   Answer: It was finally payday and the new employee got a — REALITY CHECK

5. **Jumbles:** PORCH LARVA RADIAL DROWSY
   Answer: He graduated with a degree in street building which made him a — "ROAD" SCHOLAR

6. **Jumbles:** ABIDE CLOTH UNWISE SAVORY
   Answer: After he stole second, the baseball players — TOUCHED BASE

7. **Jumbles:** NOTCH TINGE BESIDE ARTERY
   Answer: The campground's population goes up when people become — "INHABIT-TENTS"

8. **Jumbles:** ADAPT DUNCE SALMON LIKELY
   Answer: Her allergies were acting up on her tropical vacation. She felt like she was in — "POLLEN-ESIA"

9. **Jumbles:** RUGBY OMEGA ROTARY SPOTTY
   Answer: When the macaws put on a play, it was a — "PARROTY"

10. **Jumbles:** ADOPT INEPT LESSON INLAND
    Answer: She wanted her husband to take out the trash, but he considered himself to be — INDISPOSED

11. **Jumbles:** CYCLE HOLLY ARCADE BOTANY
    Answer: After sinking the winning basket, he and his teammates — HAD A BALL

12. **Jumbles:** DEPTH AGAIN OBLONG BEMOAN
    Answer: The kids wanted to play baseball, but there weren't enough gloves — ON HAND

13. **Jumbles:** TEMPO TARDY STORMY GRAVEL
    Answer: The dog knew which stores to get snacks at because he was "TREAT" SMART

14. **Jumbles:** ARENA VERGE OUTLAW SPHINX
    Answer: The poet didn't specialize in any one type of poetry because he was — "VERSE-ATILE"

15. **Jumbles:** ADAGE RIVER ENSIGN ADVICE
    Answer: The golfers loved their new electric car, especially its — DRIVING RANGE

16. **Jumbles:** ADMIT VENUE ARGYLE BEHOLD
    Answer: The zombie couple worried that their son was becoming a — DEADBEAT

17. **Jumbles:** ABIDE PRICE VELVET RARITY
    Answer: The weather forecast ended up being incorrect, which was — PREDICTABLE

18. **Jumbles:** STUNG CRIMP EATERY EXODUS
    Answer: He couldn't train for the marathon because his cold had to — RUN ITS COURSE

19. **Jumbles:** WHILE RATIO IGUANA ICONIC
    Answer: For the fashion model, always being on a diet and counting calories was — WEARING THIN

20. **Jumbles:** YEAST SILKY INVEST PELVIC
    Answer: She planned on finishing her lollipop — LICKETY-SPLIT

21. **Jumbles:** GRIPE SENSE UPROAR RADIUS
    Answer: Since their last trip to the Czech Republic capital, there'd been much — "PRAGUE-RESS"

22. **Jumbles:** DIGIT GUEST SHRINK SEWAGE
    Answer: He was hoping to get a royal flush, but the cards didn't quite — SUIT HIS NEEDS

23. **Jumbles:** AGENT DOOZY ENGULF BOTHER
    Answer: When she reached the rim of the Grand Canyon, she was — ON EDGE

24. **Jumbles:** OPERA BLAND GRILLE ENCORE
    Answer: The canine wanted to be stationed between Canada and the U.S. because he was a — BORDER COLLIE

25. **Jumbles:** COVET GEESE TANGLE INDUCT
    Answer: The chef's new high-tech knife was — CUTTING EDGE

26. **Jumbles:** BOTCH RISKY CINDER ALLEGE
    Answer: The surfers were having a wonderful time. Everything was — "BEACHY"-KEEN

27. **Jumbles:** PERCH AWAIT STUDIO SYSTEM
    Answer: The cookies shaped like tennis rackets were a hit. Everyone really liked their — SWEET SPOTS

28. **Jumbles:** OFTEN KIOSK IMMUNE COUSIN
    Answer: Farley rolled on the barn floor because of his — "IN-STINKS"

29. **Jumbles:** FAULT NINTH WEIGHT DISMAY
    Answer: When the plane hit turbulence, everything — WENT FLYING

30. **Jumbles:** TRUNK DRESS SHAKEN BECOME
    Answer: To paint the swimmers, the artist used — BRUSH STROKES

31. **Jumbles:** VIRUS VITAL PARADE OPENLY
    Answer: There was a rumor going around that she was a witch . . . She wanted to — "DISPELL" IT

32. **Jumbles:** ORBIT UNDUE ENCORE BURLAP
    Answer: When it started to rain hard during the baseball game, the fans — POURED OUT

33. **Jumbles:** UTTER WIPER BARBER APIECE
    Answer: They watched the video featuring the female sheep on — "EWE"-TUBE

34. **Jumbles:** STUFF DAISY TRIVIA KENNEL
    Answer: They couldn't figure out why the woman had passed out . . . They didn't have the — FAINTEST IDEA

35. **Jumbles:** CABLE FUSSY NUGGET POTATO
    Answer: Trying to find their misplaced map was a — LOST CAUSE

36. **Jumbles:** QUEST GULCH INDUCT LAZILY
    Answer: After a long day, the telemarketer was ready to — CALL IT QUITS

37. **Jumbles:** UNIFY PRICE TIGHTS OUTLET
    Answer: After signing a huge contract, the fashion model was — SITTING PRETTY

38. **Jumbles:** UNFIT RIGOR SEWAGE NOTION
    Answer: His story about the Liberty Bell didn't — RING TRUE

39. **Jumbles:** ABACK DODGE THROUGH REGRET
    Answer: After trying to use a stolen credit card, the identity thief was going to be — CHARGED

40. **Jumbles:** VIPER EVOKE THIRST RADIUS
    Answer: The tennis courts at the minimum security prison featured — SERVERS

41. **Jumbles:** HIKER CLIMB ATTEND LAVISH
Answer: When she quit her job as a housekeeper, she made a — CLEAN BREAK

42. **Jumbles:** UPEND HOARD ZEALOT ZOMBIE
Answer: When they carved the Jumble into the side of the mountain, they made a — HARD PUZZLE

43. **Jumbles:** VENUE RELIC FOLLOW UTOPIA
Answer: Leaving his electric car plugged in all night made it — "POWER-FULL"

44. **Jumbles:** CANAL BRAVE UTMOST INTENT
Answer: When asked how a smaller opponent had pulverized him, the boxer said — BEATS ME

45. **Jumbles:** THEFT USHER COMEDY BYPASS
Answer: The cyclops went to bed because he wanted to get — SOME SHUT-EYE

46. **Jumbles:** LEMUR KNELT HAMPER CAMPUS
Answer: The computer programmer with the bad cold was a — HACKER

47. **Jumbles:** UNWED APART HEALTH ENOUGH
Answer: When the twins went to the park to play, they went — "TWO-GETHER"

48. **Jumbles:** AMUSE TOOTH THRILL FLAWED
Answer: They were enjoying the all-you-can-eat steak restaurant — TO THE FULLEST

49. **Jumbles:** LUNCH HILLY FIBULA PUNDIT
Answer: After their air conditioner broke down again, she wished her husband could take a — CHILL PILL

50. **Jumbles:** POKER TRUNK AGENCY PONCHO
Answer: Sylvester Stallone wanted to go for a relaxing swim at the beach, but it was — TOO ROCKY

51. **Jumbles:** EXTOL HUMID FIGURE FLATLY
Answer: What the working mom considered her exercise hour — "FLEX" TIME

52. **Jumbles:** OUTDO BRIBE INDUCE FUMBLE
Answer: Why the lawyers lost to the accountants — THEY WERE OUTNUMBERED

53. **Jumbles:** PRUNE ROACH CHISEL GLANCE
Answer: What he was considered in the sales marathon — A SHOE-IN

54. **Jumbles:** KNELL ADAGE RECTOR BEDECK
Answer: What happened to the sailor who missed his ship? — HE WAS "DOCKED"

55. **Jumbles:** LEAVE RAINY JETSAM SAVAGE
Answer: How the photographer achieved positive results — WITH NEGATIVES

56. **Jumbles:** BANDY GUILD CARNAL INFECT
Answer: That sneaky accountant got the promotion because he was — "CALCULATING"

57. **Jumbles:** WOVEN SORRY SCORCH UNSAID
Answer: What the puzzle-maker had for his assistant — CROSS WORDS

58. **Jumbles:** CUBIC UPPER KITTEN MENACE
Answer: What the guests considered the baker's masterpiece — A PIECE OF CAKE

59. **Jumbles:** CHAIR DOUGH ITALIC UNTRUE
Answer: When the pool player took his turn he was — RIGHT ON CUE

60. **Jumbles:** SHAKY MOSSY HARBOR BELLOW
Answer: When they didn't win the balloon race they were known as — "SOAR" LOSERS

61. **Jumbles:** TROTH SIEGE NAUGHT INVOKE
Answer: What King Arthur's girl said before they parted — "NIGHT, KNIGHT"

62. **Jumbles:** VISTA BLIMP ENCAMP FLAXEN
Answer: They adored the horn player because he had — "SAX APPEAL"

63. **Jumbles:** BOUGH TRUTH POLICY CAMPUS
Answer: What the couple called their tennis dates — A COURTSHIP

64. **Jumbles:** HURRY SOOTY FERRET SHOULD
Answer: What linemen call the minutes in a football game — "RUSH" HOUR

65. **Jumbles:** OFTEN PRIZE VOLUME HIATUS
Answer: How they described their cornfield adventure — "LOST IN THE MAIZE"

66. **Jumbles:** LUNGE ERASE ATTAIN LIZARD
Answer: How the passers-by found the demonstration — ARRESTING

67. **Jumbles:** PAUSE UNWED HALVED NEPHEW
Answer: How the pitcher felt after he was sent to the showers — ALL WASHED UP

68. **Jumbles:** FOLIO SWOOP BOUNTY MARLIN
Answer: When you cheat on your diet the result can be — "WAIST"-FULL

69. **Jumbles:** RODEO TASTY COMPLY NUDISM
Answer: How the loggers left the forest — STUMPED

70. **Jumbles:** BRAWL LARVA DECODE VENDOR
Answer: When the elevator got stuck, it was this — A "DOWNER"

71. **Jumbles:** HOIST MESSY TROPHY BLUING
Answer: One who forges — a common name — SMITH

72. **Jumbles:** BALKY MANLY CODGER ZINNIA
Answer: Famous Middle East "strip" — GAZA

73. **Jumbles:** HASTY RANCH BETAKE ITALIC
Answer: Where the champ's "purse" ended up — IN HERS

74. **Jumbles:** BLOAT FANCY SWERVE DEFAME
Answer: This kind of money might come from a stone — "NOTES"

75. **Jumbles:** DUNCE WHISK ARMORY BROKEN
Answer: What to wear to avoid blows — A WINDBREAKER

76. **Jumbles:** ACRID WINCE JACKET SMUDGE
Answer: Sounds like a funny break — A "WISE CRACK"

77. **Jumbles:** VALOR DIZZY CALIPH GARLIC
Answer: Keep away from this empty space! — "A-VOID"

78. **Jumbles:** DEMON BANJO VORTEX MATRON
Answer: Go there if you're crazy about it! — "OVERBOARD"

79. **Jumbles:** SHEAF MEALY ABSORB HUNTER
Answer: Put on some fat! — BASTE

80. **Jumbles:** YACHT RUSTY DELUGE JANGLE
Answer: Trying — in a box — THE JURY

81. **Jumbles:** MINOR SKIMP EXHORT GARISH
Answer: What a seal might make — AN IMPRESSION

82. **Jumbles:** QUIRE LINEN POLICY CHORUS
Answer: What they called the British beef tycoon — "SIR LOIN"

83. **Jumbles:** ELUDE DRAFT POLLEN FEDORA
Answer: How he felt when pushed off the diving board — "OFF-ENDED"

84. **Jumbles:** CYCLE FORGO DIMITY POISON
Answer: What the quarreling musicians settled — AN OLD SCORE

85. **Jumbles:** BEFOG INLET HICCUP LIQUOR
Answer: It's quite a job — let there be no bones about it! — FILLETING

86. **Jumbles:** COWER FAULT BALLAD MAGNET
Answer: What you're apt to find up a policeman's sleeve — THE ARM OF THE LAW

87. **Jumbles:** VERVE COUPE TIMELY BONNET
    Answer: Lose it and you'll have nothing to say —
    YOUR VOICE

88. **Jumbles:** RABBI IMBUE SLOGAN INVERT
    Answer: Tell them when no one believes it! — THE MARINES

89. **Jumbles:** FEIGN EXCEL TARTAR HELPER
    Answer: What's in this stands out — RELIEF

90. **Jumbles:** FORAY GUILT BRANDY EMPLOY
    Answer: Flies to give warning — A RED FLAG

91. **Jumbles:** NEWLY ELITE BANTER SHAKEN
    Answer: What life under canvas might be —
    INTENSE (in tents)

92. **Jumbles:** YOUTH FOLIO BUBBLE FEWEST
    Answer: A party where some guests might be extinguished
    — A BLOWOUT

93. **Jumbles:** FISHY LAPEL PAYOFF MEDLEY
    Answer: Has a prominent position in the country — A HILL

94. **Jumbles:** HIKER DROOP BANGLE VANISH
    Answer: Why it's cheaper to eat out of doors —
    NO OVERHEAD

95. **Jumbles:** BOOTH CREEK MODEST BUTANE
    Answer: It's HARD to get as low as this — ROCK BOTTOM

96. **Jumbles:** ONION HARPY ALKALI VIRILE
    Answer: This bird cheats at cards — A ROOK

97. **Jumbles:** GAUGE BIPED NOUGAT INLAID
    Answer: Could be the subject of a tender attachment —
    AN ENGINE

98. **Jumbles:** ACUTE KEYED LIQUID FORGOT
    Answer: Stripped — in a sheepish way — FLEECED

99. **Jumbles:** MIDGE GAUZE ZITHER ORIGIN
    Answer: A course taken by people who overdo it — ZIGZAG

100. **Jumbles:** GUILE BEGUN DOOMED PIRACY
     Answer: "Just a little bit on top" — "GOING BALD"

101. **Jumbles:** PAYEE TOOTH VESTRY FLATLY
     Answer: Obviously not right from the start —
     LEFT AT THE POST

102. **Jumbles:** JUDGE MANGY DECODE TIMING
     Answer: Old-fashioned but seems to have plenty of
     boyfriends — "DATED"

103. **Jumbles:** KNACK OPIUM PASTRY CONVEX
     Answer: Took in crowds — THE PICKPOCKET

104. **Jumbles:** BILGE SKULK LAXITY TREMOR
     Answer: Keep it and you won't move! — STILL

105. **Jumbles:** YODEL MOUSY WHALER GUTTER
     Answer: They sound catty — "MEOWS"

106. **Jumbles:** MINUS FEWER HAWKER IMBIBE
     Answer: A conclusion one might make at church — "AMEN"

107. **Jumbles:** MOURN YIELD ASSURE ROSARY
     Answer: Where to look for a helping hand —
     THE END OF YOUR ARM

108. **Jumbles:** CYNIC VENOM ARTERY MYOPIC
     Answer: When the bartender's away there should be
     another… — ON TAP

109. **Jumbles:** BLAZE MOUND FACADE UNEASY
     Answer: How the loser ran — "ALSO"

110. **Jumbles:** STUNG OXIDE CIRCUS SICKEN
     Answer: TEN SONS might COMPOSE these poems —
     "SONNETS"

111. **Jumbles:** MOUNT AXIOM SYSTEM CELERY
     Answer: May be used as an opening for a letter — STEAM

112. **Jumbles:** CRESS MOUTH VACANT THRUSH
     Answer: Many people tear 'em out of books — MATCHES

113. **FOUNT SPURN PUDDLE COWARD**
     Answer: Why he couldn't get off the bus —
     IT WAS "NONSTOP"

114. **Jumbles:** COMET VIRUS DEPUTY AERATE
     Answer: What one shot sometimes starts — A RACE

115. **Jumbles:** SHINY CLOVE INTAKE TERROR
     Answer: No veins in this kind of meat — VENISON

116. **Jumbles:** HAREM MERGE BRIDLE OPPOSE
     Answer: It's not difficult to do things with it — EASE

117. **Jumbles:** CROAK TOXIN SLEIGH BUTTER
     Answer: Sounds like light music — A TORCH SONG

118. **Jumbles:** CIVIL GUARD HAUNCH DRUDGE
     Answer: Her capacity is 8 pints — A GAL.

119. **Jumbles:** BROOK ANNOY MOSQUE BLITHE
     Answer: Sometimes played in one's absence — HOOKY

120. **Jumbles:** SYLPH ICING BOUNTY UPWARD
     Answer: Pays an informal visit when dad's home — POPS IN

121. **Jumbles:** PROVE WIPED BOTANY URCHIN
     Answer: PRANCED around with a RED CAPE — "CAPE-RED"

122. **Jumbles:** BALMY PIVOT AROUND FORMAT
     Answer: Not kept in the dark — "TOLD"

123. **Jumbles:** PRUNE AVAIL BUTTON LETHAL
     Answer: Fold in cloth — A PLEAT

124. **Jumbles:** LUCID BEGOT VIOLIN ASYLUM
     Answer: It's not clear what's been written… — ILLEGIBLY

125. **Jumbles:** JOUST TANGY BUTLER WHENCE
     Answer: They help to keep the tent up — THE "GUYS"

126. **Jumbles:** TRILL PIOUS LIBIDO WEASEL
     Answer: What you might do over the eyes — PULL WOOL

127. **Jumbles:** CROON APRON PAUPER TRIBAL
     Answer: What to drink coming out of a trance — NECTAR

128. **Jumbles:** MOLDY ARDOR COUPLE BLOODY
     Answer: This dashing young man is a mere boy inside! —
     A "B-LAD-E"

129. **Jumbles:** MIRTH AZURE NEWEST JETSAM
     Answer: Stop — then charge! — ARREST

130. **Jumbles:** OLDER CRAZY MARVEL GROUCH
     Answer: Long ago there were days of it — "YORE"

131. **Jumbles:** POUND WOMEN QUENCH LACKEY
     Answer: Where a waiter might find a good tip —
     ON A NEW PEN

132. **Jumbles:** ANKLE CRANK DEAFEN GIMLET
     Answer: Where to go in and cast a spell — "ENTRANCE"

133. **Jumbles:** IMPEL CARGO FIESTA INTENT
     Answer: More agreeable — with ice in it! — "N-ICE-R"

134. **Jumbles:** POWER APPLY ENCAMP MISLAY
     Answer: Shows what the rest ought to be like — A SAMPLE

135. **Jumbles:** AGENT MAKER FLAUNT SIPHON
     Answer: "The boat's back!" — STERN

136. **Jumbles:** CLOAK LEGAL RARELY FICKLE
     Answer: Might ring his neck! — A COLLAR

137. **Jumbles:** MINCE SUEDE PIGEON FACTOR
     Answer: They may give you ideas — AIDES

138. **Jumbles:** FELON GRIMY BEAUTY GLOOMY
     Answer: Sometimes taken out shopping — but not always
     — MONEY

139. **Jumbles:** CAMEO STOOP KNIGHT ENAMEL
     Answer: When might he keep his word? —
     WHEN NO ONE TAKES IT

140. **Jumbles:** ENEMY PIANO CHOSEN INJURE
     Answer: These stories only SOUND like they're slow-moving
     — CREEPY ONES

141. **Jumbles:** PHONY MAJOR CAVIAR FUMBLE
     Answer: This bird won't steal out — A "ROB-IN"

142. **Jumbles:** ROACH MAGIC ECZEMA PICNIC
Answer: Straight from the shoulder! — AN ARM

143. **Jumbles:** PARTY OCCUR CAMPUS KIMONO
Answer: You might change coats for this opera! — "TOSCA"

144. **Jumbles:** GUILD NOBLE MARROW DOMINO
Answer: A touching reminder — A NUDGE

145. **Jumbles:** HEAVY FLOUR WIDEST NINETY
Answer: Why the biggest animal leaves no footprints — THE WHALE HAS NO FEET

146. **Jumbles:** ENTRY QUAKE TURKEY CENSUS
Answer: In short — sit down!" — "SQUAT"

147. **Jumbles:** FINAL DRAMA MIDWAY EXODUS
Answer: Must be taken in water — A SWIM

148. **Jumbles:** WHEEL BERET LAGOON OBTUSE
Answer: Where some people manage to keep their weight down — BELOW THE BELT

149. **Jumbles:** DELVE CRAWL LEEWAY EXHALE
Answer: One might be relieved to say it! — "WHEW"

150. **Jumbles:** WHEAT CASTE HOPPER ANYWAY
Answer: May be pressed for time — A STOPWATCH

151. **Jumbles:** GRIEF NOISY FAMOUS INJECT
Answer: How odd that it might be square! — A RING

152. **Jumbles:** ALBUM SORRY PRISON TIPTOE
Answer: This composer had America right in him! — "SO-U.S.A."

153. **Jumbles:** ELOPE AISLE SCENIC IMPEDE
Answer: Put down to come up — SEEDS

154. **Jumbles:** SMOKY CHAIR DEPICT LEGACY
Answer: They'd be expected to leave eggs — CHICKS

155. **Jumbles:** PAUSE IVORY FELONY MORBID
Answer: Smack 'em just for pure enjoyment — YOUR LIPS

156. **Jumbles:** GRAVE FAINT ERMINE PEOPLE
Answer: A person without male offspring — "A PER"

157. **Jumbles:** UNCLE DAILY INJURY BAMBOO
Answer: A well-known club for gymnasts — AN INDIAN CLUB

158. **Jumbles:** LILAC THICK BAKERY FAUCET
Answer: There's a catch to this one! — A LATCH

159. **Jumbles:** POISE SOLAR MALTED WORTHY
Answer: What the proverbial carpenter had a collection of — OLD SAWS

160. **Jumbles:** LOUSE CHESS TYPHUS MOHAIR
Answer: A piece of Chopin suitable at dinnertime — "CHOP"

161. **Jumbles:** FOURTH GAZEBO ABACUS WEAKLY AROUND EXOTIC
Answer: The zebras stopped by to visit the giraffes when they were in the giraffes' — NECK OF THE WOODS

162. **Jumbles:** INLAND DEFECT HIGHLY ROCKET FERVOR UPDATE
Answer: The ski lift to the top of the mountain was so popular because of its — PEAK EFFICIENCY

163. **Jumbles:** TACKLE ENOUGH ALWAYS UPROAR CURFEW INCOME
Answer: The new grocery store was so successful thanks to its — SUPER MARKETING

164. **Jumbles:** INHALE STEREO SLEIGH MEEKLY GROUCH ABRUPT
Answer: After the student disrupted the class, the teacher — TAUGHT HIM A LESSON

165. **Jumbles:** WORTHY ENTICE SEPTIC DISMAY SONATA INDICT
Answer: When the zombie went swimming, he was — DEAD IN THE WATER

166. **Jumbles:** EXPAND FLAVOR DETECT EUREKA VISION APIECE
Answer: Even though it's a road race, the Indianapolis 500 is a — TRACK-AND-FIELD EVENT

167. **Jumbles:** MORTAL NAPKIN OUTAGE CHOSEN THEORY AMBUSH
Answer: The bodybuilder wasn't going to have any luck with the woman because he — CAME ON TOO STRONG

168. **Jumbles:** INFAMY HOURLY DETACH JESTER ACTIVE MISHAP
Answer: When he saw an opportunity to win a free skydiving lesson, he — JUMPED AT THE CHANCE

169. **Jumbles:** WALLOP TANDEM SHADOW SUPERB NAPKIN WEAKLY
Answer: The forest ranger's job was a — WALK IN THE PARK

170. **Jumbles:** TOMATO UNDONE GOALIE UPROAR BIOPSY COLUMN
Answer: Finishing first in the marathon created a — LASTING MEMORY

171. **Jumbles:** GAINED MOSQUE RARITY CIRCUS SHERRY DITHER
Answer: When the school band got stuck in traffic, they — USED THEIR HORNS

172. **Jumbles:** GUNNER TRUSTY IMPEDE ORCHID PARISH OFFSET
Answer: What he said when he bought the $50 perfume — NOT A "SCENT" MORE

173. **Jumbles:** FOSSIL GARBLE ENMITY INVENT MOBILE TOFFEE
Answer: What the quarterback's nasty pass protectors were known as — AN "OFFENSIVE" LINE

174. **Jumbles:** FALLEN VELVET RELISH WHENCE PAUPER VESTRY
Answer: When the actress visited the doctor in her movie role, she — WASN'T "HERSELF"

175. **Jumbles:** FIASCO BOUGHT DETACH POLITE SHADOW REBUKE
Answer: When many didn't suit her, she remained — WITHOUT A SUITOR

176. **Jumbles:** PENCIL BANNER INBORN BASKET PRIMER CANDID
Answer: Why the engineer stayed singularly focused on his work — HE HAD A ONE TRACK MIND

177. **Jumbles:** COUPON EXPOSE NATURE SAVORY AROUSE JERSEY
Answer: What the bungling photographer got at the beach — OVER EXPOSURE

178. **Jumbles:** ECZEMA DREDGE GLOBAL VIABLE BECKON MARROW
Answer: How did the cowboy beat the heat? — HE RODE BAREBACK

179. **Jumbles:** RATION DEMURE NOODLE BAZAAR PLENTY BIGAMY
Answer: Guaranteed to put you to sleep — A "BORED" MEETING

180. **Jumbles:** BYWORD PAGODA MARVEL BECAME FONDLY SONATA
Answer: What the bicycling entrepreneur did — HE "PEDDLED" HIS WARES